The
Lessons
I Learned

*Bring Back Old-School Communication
to Succeed in Business*

PAUL R. BECKER

authorHOUSE®

AuthorHouse™
1663 Liberty Drive
Bloomington, IN 47403
www.authorhouse.com
Phone: 1 (800) 839-8640

Published by AuthorHouse 11/13/2017

ISBN: 978-1-5462-1605-6 (sc)
ISBN: 978-1-5462-1603-2 (hc)
ISBN: 978-1-5462-1604-9 (e)

Library of Congress Control Number: 2017917270

Print information available on the last page.

Dedicated to the person I have spent the last eighteen years of my life with, the person I shared fortunes with and made plans for our future. Through good times and bad, the bond between us has become stronger. Let's see what our future holds and if these fortunes become reality.

Thank you, Kyle.

INTRODUCTION

Through many life events, I reflect back to my upbringing and search for lessons I learned that will inspire others to succeed. Early on, I began to build a network of family and friends who would support my decisions along the way. There have been road bumps and moments of self-reflection, but at this point, I am proud.

I wrote my story to inspire people to express their feelings and certainly get back to talking. We all have so much to say, and one simple gesture of listening would make a difference. Put down social media for a time and get back to enjoying each other.

Never be afraid to ask questions and express your opinions. Share your thoughts and let people know you have a voice. There are times to be silent, but getting noticed requires a voice.

The people who influence your life will hold a special spot forever.

Our careers are important, and we should focus on goals that will take us to the next level. You hold that power in your hand, and if you know how to use those tools, the world is yours to concur.

This book is to inspire our young generation to take charge of their careers and understand the path previous generations have taken to succeed. It's about communication and taking time to reflect and understand how different our lives can be.

I want to touch managers who are struggling with staffing issues and hiring practices to better grasp how the future generation will impact business. We need to take control and guide our future leaders and those who will step in our shoes someday.

There is nothing wrong with reflecting back on the past and learning from the teachings our parents and family instilled on us.

Good luck.

CHAPTER 1

So It Begins

I started this journey fifty-four years ago, and through many bumps in the road, I have come to a place to stop, reflect, and share my thoughts before I begin the final journey: the remaining years of my life. Some people say they could never live a long life; they don't want to age. I find that selfish because I want to live as long as I can and, of course, be as healthy as I can be too. I want to see my own family grow and be a part of their lives to share my stories of success and failures, the same as my grandparents did many years ago.

When I look back at my childhood, I can honestly say I have no regrets. Sure, I made mistakes, pick the wrong friends, or shut out the good friends we got mad at for a stupid reason. Of course at the time, we thought the reason seemed good, but now, maybe not. If I have a regret, it's not being able to hit Rewind sometimes. I would like to live some of those special moments over and over.

As kids, our feelings got hurt for silly reasons. We said things that were not necessarily true, and we tried to stretch the truth. We were creative in making up stories to stretch the truth—not to hurt anyone—but we used our imaginations. I would never encourage people to lie to each other.

Think about past conversations on the front porches of our parents' homes, in the backyard, or on bike rides to the local store with our childhood friends. We talked about our plans to be a doctor, teacher, or the next all-star athlete. On those bike rides, we used to pretend our bikes were the newest Cadillacs or a sports car we saw on TV. Growing up, we had imaginations; we had fun turning that two-wheeler into our first car or truck. Do you remember clipping playing cards onto your wheel spokes so your bike made a cool sound? It was fun using our imaginations and simple things at our disposal to enhance our experiences; we still remember them today. At least, I remember.

In the evenings, we sat as a family and had dinner at the table; we talked about our day and listened as our parents advised us. Mom and Dad were cool then. I remember helping to clear the table and asking my parents what our plans were for the weekend. Of course, they included visiting grandparents, having dinner together, and being a family. It's funny to think back and remember "making plans," "family," "together," and "listening." I rarely hear those words today.

As the days grew into months and those months into years, it seemed our childhood lessons and experiences quickly moved into young adulthood. Those long years of preschool and grade school now seemed like they never happened, but in the moment, I counted down the years until I could drive. In those years, we chose our friends because we wanted to be accepted at the cool lunch table. It was easier then because no one judged you for how you dressed or the bad haircut your mother gave you. Speaking of dress, I remember my parents telling me I could not go to school without a tie on. I was also into plaid. Okay, well, that has not changed, but at least I don't wear a tie.

Even as children, we looked to the future and never seemed to accept the current moment. Is that how we are programmed from the beginning? At that point, we wanted to know more, but that was normal for young adults back then. Our family values were drilled into our minds, and the expectations for our future still had to be determined.

CHAPTER 2

Growin' Up

I remember wondering what the next floor of the school was like. As we moved from grade to grade, it was our goal to get on those upper floors. As you moved up, you earned more respect, and now I was there. I was one of the cool kids. Or so I thought. I had the same friends but with a new look and different attitudes. Young adulthood brought a lot of questions about who I was and what I wanted to do with myself. *Do I plan my future, and will I know what the right path is for me?* So many questions and so little time to think it all through.

Those conversations around our dreams began to focus on reality. My bike was no longer the new Cadillac; it was just my bike that I used to ride to the store for Mom. I now had responsibilities. I was growing up. Going to the store gave me the responsibility of making sure I only bought what was on Mom's list, and she knew the costs too. Mom wanted the receipt, and if I decided to buy some penny candy, I had to budget that in. Sure— she would always give me an extra buck or two.

I used to dream of my first real job. I remember looking at cars with my dad and thinking that I would own the latest model someday. He and I would drive out to different dealerships on Sunday afternoons and look at the cars and compare prices and colors. It was our time to bond, which I value to this day. I am certain not many fathers and sons have that type of bond today. Kids are hung up on video games and don't use their imaginations. Do they even dream? We all have dreams, whether we are young or old. Some, of course, we want to forget, but others we cherish for a lifetime. As we looked at each new model of car, I would fantasize about the color combination I wanted and all the extras. In those days, you were lucky to get power windows.

I cannot imagine the millennials having to manually roll their windows down or move their seats to adjust them. If only we could send people back in time.

My ultimate dream was thinking about my first apartment and moving out to share a place to live with my friend: staying up late, going out for dinner, and eating anything I wanted. But in some ways, I knew those were dreams because right then, I wanted everything to stay the same. Living at home was my safety, and I liked it.

For some reason, my friends began to be busy with other things. There was no time for those long talks about what life would be like. We had a social life now. We had responsibilities, which came to be known as chores. Watching Dad cut grass from the front porch was over; I was doing it now. Dad was on the porch watching me and drinking an ice cold beer. *Beer!* When will that happen? Mom had chores for me too. I helped with cleaning or taking laundry to the basement. Washing cars was the ultimate.

I never had fears for the future; it all seemed exciting. I knew life would be kind, but would it go smoothly? At that point in life, we all expected smooth sailing. I had life by the balls, and it was mine to live.

Was I truly prepared for the next phase of life? Honestly, I was not. I had feelings of fear, anxiety, and uncertainty. I think that's normal for anyone. You can never predict what comes next, but I had it in my mind I could control every aspect of it.

In elementary school, things seemed to be secure because the same classmates I started with in first grade continued on the journey with me. We were a team; on occasion, a new player joined it, but not often. We helped each other through so many life events. It was a family, and I feared what would happen after eighth grade. There were choices to make, and I knew my choice was not one that I would welcome.

CHAPTER 3

Moving On

The people I grew up with and spent eight years of my childhood with moved on to another high school, and that was hard for me to accept. We said goodbye and went in different directions. I was alone now, thinking I had to work hard and start over building friendships. I had never really known the emotion of loneliness until now. I was scared. But I had to tell myself it was only four years, and if I had made it through eight, I could do this.

Talking to my parents about my first day at a new high school made it somewhat better, but I was not happy. I remember thinking that I had to endure this hell for four years. It was not easy, and I hated every day. After eight years of a Catholic grade school, I was now into another four years in a Catholic high school. That was not the entire issue, but it played a part.

During this transition, my dad became devoted to the Catholic church. He was ordained a deacon in our parish and the city of Pittsburgh. So what would this mean to my sister and me? I had so many questions and was proud of him. But I sensed changes in our family, and it would include our church. This was a commitment for him and for us too.

In my mind, I related this to "Sit, Stand, and Kneel." Not just on Sunday but on every holiday, dedication Mass, and holy day—sometime multiple times during the week. At one point I thought, *Is this reality?* Back then, we could have created a reality show. Good thing the Kardashians weren't around then. The name of my show would have been *Sit, Stand, Kneel with the Beckers.*

Of course I was the rebel; I pushed the button and asked a lot of questions. Not that I did much to cause issues, but I wanted to understand things. The icing on the cake was our parish priest came on vacations with us. I believed and certainly said my prayers, but why did we need to have Sunday services in our hotel room? Oh, and we used Town Talk bread as our hosts. Really? That is the point I started to wonder and began to ask questions. Even though I was young and still learning, I knew my time would be limited in this religious upbringing. I had to know.

So eight years of Catholic grade school, and now four years of Catholic high school. Was this really who I would become? Was I on the path to begin a religious life of Sit, Stand, and Kneel? Nope. It was not for me, but I do respect anyone who chooses that life. I can see how people get wrapped up in the community; it has to become an individual choice.

On Saturday evenings, my father used to write his Sunday homilies at the dining room table. He would write and rewrite the words until he was able to effectively communicate it without reading word for word on Sunday. Of course we had to attend the Mass he was speaking at: family support. My mind would drift back to my dreams and what I had planned for the day. I could never concentrate enough to grasp the concept. Maybe it was the repetitive words every Sunday that never seemed to change and we were programmed to recite.

As I got settled in a routine and became more familiar with my new surroundings in high school, I was able to settle in for the next adventure. I made friends and had a close group that I spent time with. They were cool. I took time to learn the ins and outs of school and got myself familiar with who were the outcasts. I was not a jock or a geek, so I fit in the middle. I learned early on to keep all groups in my network, whether I fit in or not. I was playing the game to survive.

I had great times with friends, but now it was time to get a part-time job. I wanted to make money. My first job was at an ice cream shop near where I grew up. It was clear from day one I was not going to be behind the counter making cones; I was immediately escorted to the kitchen and told to scrub the dirty pots and pans. So I was not the soda jerk. I was the kitchen help. I remember getting my first paycheck and could not decide what I wanted to buy. I think my first big purchase was a new shirt for school. That's when I started to get my own sense of style.

I stayed for some time but wanted a new career. So I applied for a job at a shoe store. It seemed to be a little more glamorous; at least my hands were not soaked in dirty grease water all night. The plus side was I got to wear a tie every day. Now that was cool. I learned the business and was working the register. My manager now wanted to train me on inventory. That came with a new appreciation for adult magazines. The manager had a vast collection at his desk in the back room. They opened my eyes up to new things. My mind raced but that Catholic upbringing was saying "Sit, Stand, and Kneel." Oh, that Catholic guilt gets you every time.

Honestly, I would eat my lunch at his desk just so I could glance at those magazines.

After several months, it was time for a new adventure. There was an ad in our local paper for a fast food clerk. A new mall was opening, and the restaurant was looking to hire. I called, set up an interview, and immediately got the job. Training in two weeks. So this was the first time I really understood the need of giving your employer notice. I realized I had to tell them but never got the idea of two weeks. Made sense.

When I got to work and gave my notice, the butterflies in my stomach were going crazy. I was never so nervous. I did understand that was the right thing to do, and I was following protocol. I guess I was not sure how my boss would feel, but then I realized it must happen often because people move on. I obviously got the job when someone resigned, so it's the way it goes.

My first day on the new job was so exciting: a brand-new store and people I never met in my life. In some way, we all had something in common. I fit in here. Training was scheduled for 8:30 a.m., and I was ten minutes early. The manager told me to wash my hands and someone would be by to get me started. Did you need to wash your hands to run a register?

So my first experience was fileting raw chicken. Was that in the job description? Soon, a second new hire joined me, and we began talking about this experience. I just kept thinking, *This is a job, and I am making money.* I did the job and finally moved to other tasks, including working the front end.

I worked hard and handled any shift I was put on: Some evenings and weekends, but since I was still in high school, I only worked a limited number of days. That was good with me. Eventually, I worked my way up

CHAPTER 4

Choices

P rom season came and went. I went to high school dances, assemblies, and the occasional date to the movies. My friends were more important, but having a steady girl looked good too. At least to my family, friends, and coworkers. We want to fit into a mold growing up that best fits everyone else. Even our families try to gear us toward a standard format of what life should look like. As young adults, we need to grasp our existence and become the drivers for the future. I realize it's hard to do, or we never think about it, but honestly, it helps your futures. I failed to take ownership and let other influences take over, and I was doing my best to go along with it.

It was now time to take another leap toward my future. Four years of high school seemed to go fast, but no fast enough. Those four years were the worst; I could never explain to anyone how I truly felt. Each day was harder than the next. In my mind, the thought of fileting chicken seemed to relieve the pressure. Funny how we look at small tasks to ease the pressures of life. Chicken? Really? This was my place to escape and dream of bigger and better. It was therapy.

Early on, we don't know what direction we should take; how can we?

My big decision was business or self-employment? Do I pursue franchise opportunities or skate through on my experience, which would lead me to the big job? I chose business. I began the task of looking into college. I was not exactly sure if I was ready but figured I had to do it; all my friends and family were going.

I kept my job at the mall and began my adult learning, or as some call it, college. I never forgot my past and the people who I felt a close bond to.

After four years of pure disappointment, my connection with friends from the past seemed to diminish. Those I did keep in touch with became close friends for life. Some of those friends I helped to get a job fileting chicken; not sure they appreciated it. That was my first experience helping someone land employment. The rush was nice and satisfying. I helped someone. I was beginning to build a network, and I had connections. People respected my opinion enough to hire one of my friends.

After college, I worked toward landing a more secure position. I was networking and finally landed a night shift position with a financial institution in Pittsburgh. For me, that was big time. I really had no idea what the position involved, but I would give it my all. I actually went to a temp agency, and they placed me in this position. I needed a foot in the door, and this was it. I learned that applying for positions in person (especially in the 1980s) was difficult at best. From the beginning, I learned that you had to take an entry-level position and lower pay to get yourself recognized. Now the hard work starts. It was going to be a long road to success, but I was ready for the challenges.

Night shift was difficult since most of my friends worked during the day. It was an adjustment, and at this time, I was still living at home. In some ways, I enjoyed having my days free. Sometimes, those adjustments give you an opportunity to dive into yourself and understand where you are going.

During this transition, my grandparents passed away, one month apart. These were my mother's parents. I loved both of them so much and enjoyed seeing them every day. They lived a few doors down from us. After all the ceremonies were done and we took personal items from the house, I made a proposal to my parents and asked if I could rent their house. We worked out a monthly payment plan and the move began. This was a great opportunity and would teach me how to be responsible and live on my own. I planned to share it with a friend who I met while fileting chicken at the mall. He was a close friend, and I knew we could make a go of it.

He and I worked opposite shifts, which was fine; actually, it seemed to work perfectly. We had girlfriends, and on weekends, we had great parties.

At work, I was learning so much. I even got promoted to supervisor. I really thought I was climbing the corporate ladder. I knew what my priorities were and understood I had to maintain a level of professionalism.

What I struggled with was knowing when to separate yourself from the people you supervised. That was hard; I did not completely grasp that concept. At least not yet.

It was interesting to me that there would be so much controversy in a professional atmosphere. I never heard so many stories people having affairs and the occasional break-up. I never had this in my past jobs, but then again, this was corporate America.

As a supervisor, I often had to tell my subordinates they were not performing according to the bank's standards. Many did not appreciate that I was now their boss. The first time I had to meet with someone and put them on corrective action bothered me so much. I was so nervous. That conversation stuck with me for a long time. Now I understood why you pull yourself away from the people you manage. I now got it.

I became engaged to the girl I was dating. Yes, I was going to be married. Was this right? Suppressed feelings and emotions told a different story. I was struggling in my mind about my own sexuality and was unsure of the path I was supposed to take. To satisfy my upbringing the direction I took was certainly not want I wanted but want I had to do. Yep, in my head, Sit, Stand, and Kneel. I heard it playing over and over again. But I had to make my family proud. It was what you did.

Or was it? I was in control of my job and career, but when it came to my personal life, I still accepted outside influences. We were programmed that way from childhood. It was drilled into our heads that you married, had children, and lived happily ever after. I was all for happily ever after, but on my terms. It's about control more than expectation.

CHAPTER 5

Wedding Plans

The plans were coming along, and the date was set. Time was spent with both families, but it felt more like a movie than real life. Maybe an old classic like *Singing in the Rain*. The drops of rain were like pokes to my soul, telling me to dig deep. My dancing along the sidewalk with the love of my life was far away. This was a life-changing decision that I was not ready for. But I was going through the motions. Those suppressed feelings were rushing in my mind. It was my own perfect storm.

Something was wrong, and I had no clue what it was. My nerves were out of control, and I had no one to talk with. At this point, I was alone mentally. Those friends I had long talks with on bike rides to the store had grown up and moved away. I was left to make decisions that met everyone's expectations but my own. I was truly sad. Applying my skills as a supervisor did not work either because I had to keep work life and personal life separate. In those days we did not have wellness centers at work.

Two weeks before the big day, I sent my mother a card and wrote a note in it. I remember saying, "I don't know if I am making the right choice." We never talked about that note, and then I stood at the altar, waiting on my bride. We shared our "I dos," and life changed forever. The emotions running through my mind were overwhelming, I honestly wanted to run out the door. I remember thinking I could just leave and never look back. I could feel the sweat running down my back as the organist started playing "Here Comes the Bride." The music filled the church, but I only heard muffled sounds.

I went through the motions and now had a wife. I was scared and knew it was a mistake.

When I look back over the six years of marriage, I can truly say I was never happy. I led a life of lies. Over the years, I moved into new positions with the bank and continued to move up the ladder. I dove into my career as if that's who I married, not the physical person I said, "I do," with in a church that Saturday afternoon.

Marriage was a dark time in my life; friends came and went, but I did not feel compelled to get close to anyone. In my mind, I told myself this was all for Sit, Stand, and Kneel. My parents and family were proud. We never had children, and that was a sign to me. I knew otherwise I was committed to this bond that I wanted to break.

To deal with this new life and my heartache, I would close my eyes and dream it would all end. Months became years, and I lost my true self. My ambitions were slipping away, and the fight to be who I thought I would become seemed to be a fantasy. This person who I hesitantly called my wife was draining me emotionally. Now I wished we had talked about the note in that card.

I can honestly say, for six years, the thoughts of how to end this kept me up at night. It had to be over because for me, I was better than this and needed to pursue who I was.

After playing the scenario over and over in my head, the day came to take back myself. I needed to own myself again. I was taking me back. I was no longer going to let this person make me feel incredibly worthless. So I did it. I ended it, and I moved on. You know what? It felt good. Not one tear was shed for me because I knew the person I was going to become. I was free.

I would not advise anyone on how to handle a similar situation. It was about me being happy. So many people continue to live lives that make them sad just because they don't want to hurt others. Why? Our lives are important, and if you are not happy, change it. But it has to be your choice. Talk to someone and be prepared to defend your actions. The moment I knew I was on my own, I felt a huge weight off my shoulders.

The next several months involved lawyers, family members reaching out to support me, and her family making accusations of why I wanted to end the marriage. I worked through all that and kept my chin up. I took a financial blow, but I would rebuild and bounce back. This was another life lesson.

I dove back into work and now was managing a group of people. Finally, I was making a name for myself, and people were noticing the good job I was doing. In addition to my marital status changing, I applied for a position with the same company in Delaware. After a couple interviews, I was offered the position and a relocation package. The person who I would report to did his homework and found out what kind of person I was and how well I would fit into the position.

You never know who is looking at you from the outside. People talk and share stories. Regardless of which business you are in, the saying of "Never burn a bridge" is true. I have always told my employees to think about who is on the other end of that phone call or email they send in frustration. That person will know someone who could potentially have input to hiring you some day. Play the game.

It was so exciting to move to a new location, meet new people, and start my new life as a single man. This was exactly what I needed to do. Oh, and I no longer felt the pressure to Sit, Stand, and Kneel anymore. This was my show now.

The new job brought added responsibility, but I was leading a team. My insight, job knowledge, and experience helped to coach others. I was confident in my decisions. I met some interesting characters along the way. I had a pen thrown at me from across a table when I put an employee on corrective action. My supervisor was hearing impaired; that was a challenge. It was such a mix of people, and it was pretty neat. Being able to apply real-life experiences to my management skills was useful. I worked hard and was able to devote full attention to my responsibilities. The satisfaction of helping others truly gave me a sense of self-worth.

Two years into my new life, I was hit with a heavy blow: My mother passed away. That hit hard. Even though I lived out of state at the time, I spent many weekends traveling back and forth to Pittsburgh. I had to support my father, and being with family was most important. My sister and her husband and I supported our father. On the outside, Dad was strong; after all, he was the deacon, and he turned to colleagues for support. He clearly was suffering. We did everything we could for him and made sure someone checked in on him. Those days of viewings and the funeral take a toll on you. To hear people say, "She is no longer suffering," was comforting, but no one seemed to worry whether Dad was. No one ever finds the right words to say during these times, and I get that, but just spending time with someone and talking could mean so much.

It was time to head back to Delaware. I remember driving for five hours and wiping tears from my eyes for at least four of those hours. My mind was racing with what options I had and how I could continue living away from home. When it came down to it, life had to go on. We remember the good times and keep the images of those we love close in our brain.

I was building a home during this time and finally moved into it. For a long time, it had been my goal to build my own home. For many years I thought about owning a home and making my own decisions of what my expectations and outcomes would be. I stopped by every day to see the progress. It was exciting to think about furnishing my house and making it my home. On those trips to see the progress I would sit in my car and close my eyes imaging welcoming friends and family into my home. I did it and it was mine. Shortly after moving in and settling in, I woke up one night in a cold sweat, feeling overwhelmed. I saw an image of a person standing in the doorway of my bedroom. I wiped the sleep from my eyes and recognized the person standing there: It was my mother. I sat straight up in bed and could feel my heart racing. She never spoke but pointed to the staircase, which led to the front door. She slowly moved down the staircase and toward the front door; as she looked back at me before exiting, I was crying. Her image passed through the door, and I was left alone, crying on the staircase. What was she saying to me? I finally realized that she came to see that I was happy and wanted to make sure I was at peace with her passing. Although I struggled with her illness and sudden death, I soon realized it was okay to be me. She approved.

Since that experience, I often take a moment to speak with her; every time I am on an airplane, I look out the window and say, "I love you and miss you." I thank her too.

It was because of how my mother raised me that I was accomplishing my goals. I listened to my parents and was led by their direction. Of course, I had my own opinions, but I seemed to be making good choices: a good example of how we are the owners of who we are and become. It's not always a smooth road, but those bumps are the challenges we must slow down and eventually cross over.

It's never easy to say goodbye in any situation. But is it ever really final? At some point, we circle back to greet those same people. Goodbye is not final; it's just a salutation that we learned. The word has been programmed into our vocabulary but was never meant to cause sorrow.

So life moves on, and I had to get back into the groove. Of course, work does not stop. So many people were supportive of my loss at work and offered to help in any way they could. These people never met my mother but felt a connection to her through me. These are the people you want in your back pocket. I knew if I really did need something, I could count on them.

One person in particular was a true close friend. She had my back no matter what. Marilyn worked for me when I first moved to Delaware, and of course I had to make that separation between work life and personal life. However, Marilyn was different. I immediately had a connection, and I could tell from the beginning we would maintain a friendship for a long time. If you could truly love a friend, Marilyn was the one. Down the road, Marilyn would be a connection to the top spot in my network. We would help each other.

Although the road started to finally smooth out and I felt I was back on track, there was another bump. The bank notified us that our division was being sold. We met with Human Resources and were presented with our severance packages. I was more concerned about the fact I just built a home and had no idea where to go next. After fourteen years with this bank, I was unemployed.

Chapter 6

My Direction

So I woke up the following Monday morning and as I sipped my coffee, looking out the living room window, I watched my neighbors leave for work. I had an empty feeling in my stomach and found it hard to accept that I was unemployed. Since my first job doing dishes to fileting chicken in the back room at the mall, I have always worked. I was a responsible person who had a duty to be employed. I never took advantage of others and always paid my way, but this time, I might need some help.

My package paid my salary for one year, so I decided to take some time off and spend it in Pittsburgh with my father. During that time, I was actively working on making connections, and within three weeks, I had interviews scheduled, so back to Delaware I went.

Because of my reputation in the banking industry, I interviewed to manage an employee temp agency in Delaware (the same agency I used to fill positions I had at the bank). This was the first time I truly knew the importance of my network. It was paying off. I got the job, and my first big assignment was to help employees of my previous employer to find jobs. That was a bit strange for me at first, but I took it with my chin up. It was satisfying helping others find jobs. I had done that before, but now that was my job. Good thing I had some experience.

As time went on, I met with other financial institutions in the area; I met so many people and made many contacts. During one of my intake sessions with a bank looking to hire customer service reps, I met with a manager from my previous employer; he ended up there after he was displaced. After several conversations about what I was now doing and talking about my goals, he made me an offer to come work for him, and I accepted. I gave my two weeks and moved on. Since I knew eventually I would need this agency, I did not burn my bridges.

Moving to a different company was a new experience for me, especially in the financial industry, but it was nice working with people I knew. Of course, there were challenges learning new systems and procedures, but it brought with it some rewards too. I could apply what I previously knew to this job. Familiar faces always seem to add a sense of calm. In some ways, it was like a family reunion, but without Aunt Colette's famous lasagna (now there is a story).

So off to Wilmington, Delaware, I went every day. I set high expectations for myself and the teams I managed. I want to see people exceed and move on to bigger and better. As a manager, I feel that if my team fails, so do I. My job was to make sure my team was successful and ready for their next chapter. There's nothing wrong with people wanting to stay in the same job for many years if they get comfortable, but the emotional reward when someone moves into a better job is gratifying.

My own career is something I valued, especially now. Those curve balls growing up were life lessons, and I was applying that to my life. When you respect others and yourself, people react to you. My network continued to build, and I was looking for all possible connections. Of course, this was before social media took control of us. We had to work hard and communicate face-to-face with other people. There was no texting. This was in the mid-90s, when our society was on the cusp of so many changes. I remember going to Happy Hours with other managers and bankers; it was a great place to meet new people.

A few months into my new position, I was asked to assist our site in St. Louis. So I packed my bags and spent a few months traveling back and forth. This was a great opportunity that showed my flexibility and willingness to extend myself. The Customer Service team in St. Louis needed some help, and the site was preparing to move. I spent most days in St. Louis dealing with client issues and personnel concerns. The site manager and I clicked, and we worked well together.

Employee conflicts are never easy; those discussions can be rough. But I seemed to embrace them and worked my way to a reasonable solution. I worked closely with Human Resources at the previous bank and become close to the HR manager. We worked closely on so many issues that I second-guessed my career choice. Maybe an HR career was in my cards. In any event, understanding the dos and don'ts helped me. Sure, there were times when my decisions were wrong, and I had to deal with the consequences, but I tried to keep the business in mind each time.

I was asked by the site manager if I would consider a position in St. Louis, managing the team permanently. I needed advice and called my father to talk through my decision. This was a big move for me; once again, I would be alone in a town I knew nothing about. After talking it over and thinking for the next week, I said yes. I had some hesitations about moving to the Midwest because I was not certain if I would ever get visitors. Living in Delaware, my family was only five hours away and often came to visit. It's one of those sacrifices we make for our career. Let's face it. I needed to do this for my future retirement plans. I had to plan for that because life is short, and after my mother's passing, I knew I had to look out for me.

The move went as planned, and I got an apartment close to work. I went nowhere except work and home, and that weighed on me. I was lonely. Vacations were spent driving ten hours to Pittsburgh. No one in my family ever came to visit me, but my true friend from Delaware did for a weekend (I knew Marilyn would). I was homesick and knew something was not right with my father. Even though I worried about him every day, I had to keep going. One year went by, and I had to make a choice. I was lonely and could not continue in this town.

On one of my trips back to Pittsburgh, I reached out to people I knew at my original employer, a bank whose headquarters were in Pittsburgh. I knew a job was going to open and started networking immediately. I set up some lunch dates and dinners and began dropping my name.

It was 1999, and the year 2000 was coming fast. I was home with my father, preparing for the world to end (well, at least that's what everyone was preparing for).

One night, I went online and checked my email. Then I entered an AOL chat room and began conversing with someone named Kyle. Without going into a lot of detail now, that was my best day ever. This was the introduction to a new chapter in my life that would be so very fulfilling. Little did I know my future was soon going to be revealed in a couple months. More on that later.

So we partied like it was 1999. After the weekend, I headed back to St. Louis, knowing my time there was ending. The offer came, and I accepted the position to move back to Pittsburgh. I basically went full circle, back to a familiar employer and back to where I began my upbringing. To help my father, I moved back in with him, in the home I grew up in.

It was odd at first moving back into my childhood home and living with my father. I had to get used to his new life, and he had to accept mine. My father changed over the years after my mother died. On the outside, he was the same, but inside, he was depressed and suffering. He was using alcohol to help him get through those nights alone. It was so hard for me to see him taking a dark path to destruction. The nights I would get home from work and he had too much to drink were a crushing blow to my well-being. I began to think of who could help; why did no one else notice his behavior? My sister Kathleen and her husband Tim knew, but we needed support. Those people who were so concerned about it during my mother's funeral were nowhere to be found. The church he dedicated his life to left him behind. He had made choices too, but at this point, his depression was deep. Every night after driving home, I would pull into the driveway, take a deep breath, and prepare myself.

For a period of time, I found myself back to the Sunday routine of Sit, Stand, and Kneel. I was only going through the motions because my true beliefs do not rely on an institution to decide how I should live my life. I was here to ask for a sign and seek help for my father. I learned to deal with it and expressed my concerns to my father.

To help, I would log back on to AOL and hope Kyle was there. We continued the conversation from the eve of 2000 and began sharing our life story. We chatted back and forth for hours and days until finally making plans to meet in person. I immediately felt a strong connection to this person and was intrigued to finally meet him. So we decided to meet for Chinese on a Saturday evening in February.

I remember driving to our designated meeting place, thinking that this connection could change my life. My spirit felt alive again. After my marriage, I never thought of having any type of relationship.

I sat on a bench and waited for my dinner companion. I watched other patrons walk by and felt like the guy who got stood up on his first date. My nerves were taking over, and as each single person approached, I tried to imagine if that was Kyle. I had seen a picture of him on-line, but all this was new to me.

Finally, Kyle arrived, and we greeted each other and went into the Chinese restaurant. From the time we met, our conversation never skipped a beat.

Dinner went great, with wonderful conversation, and I felt a strong connection to Kyle. We talked about our childhood, discussed our siblings, and shared stories about our parents. I remember thinking that I wanted to keep talking because I was so happy. I wanted the time we were spending to slow down a bit; I did not want the check yet. The waiter brought two fortune cookies. I have saved my fortune for eighteen years. It read, "In a gentle way, you can shake the world." I wondered what that meant, but hopefully the world was going to be kind. Either way, I was ready.

On the drive home after dinner, I began preparing myself for what I would come home to. How was Dad tonight? I pulled into the driveway, took a deep breath, and walked through the front door. The house was quiet, and I could hear him snoring from the bedroom. Things were good, and I felt a sense of relief. I sat in the dark for a brief time before taking myself to bed. I needed to just be alone and reflect on this day and all that led up to it.

CHAPTER 7

I Am Out

One February evening, I met Kyle for a walk along the mountaintop overlooking the city of Pittsburgh. I went back to those long bike rides as a kid and thought about the conversations we had, planning our lives. Our walk that evening was similar. We talked and listened to each other share our emotions. Little did I know this was my future unfolding, and we were creating memories that would be shared for a lifetime.

As we walked along Grandview Avenue, we took in the view of Pittsburgh. The skyscrapers were glowing with light, and cars were zooming along the highways below us.

As the seasons changed, my relationship was growing stronger, but I knew things at home were not perfect. I was torn on how this would all correct itself or what my obligation was to my father. I am a grown man and had to do what was best for me; although it felt selfish, it was what I had to do. It was five years since my mother passed away, and we had to get back to our routines.

I made another milestone decision, and that was to move out of my childhood home and start my new life. Of course, this was not what the son of a deacon was expected to do. Although the guilt played havoc in my mind, I knew in my heart and my personal well-being I would move forward. Blessings or not, it was who I am.

At this point, I learned a valuable life lesson. Even though outside influences tend to guide us in a certain direction, we have to take responsibility and do what is best for ourselves. That's not selfish; it's life. I never want to look back and have regrets. I did that in the past, and I would not return there. Those were dark days, and I was living the truth, although it was a challenge to make sure everyone understood my direction. But then again, if we are happy, that is all that counts. And when Kyle and I moved in together, we were happy.

In any relationship, there are ups and downs, especially when you first move in together. It's the "getting to know you" period. We have all been through it. Happens in our jobs too. Friends, family, and coworkers will always challenge you or push those buttons to see how far it will take before you react. The confidence you have in yourself will be your driver. Never let them see you weak.

Kyle and I moved into a new house and quickly made it our home. Family came to visit, and we hosted our friends for fun evenings. This was the start of us looking forward to entertaining and hosting parties. Our home was also the base for social event with coworkers. Now the inner circle of my network began to bond.

Even though I was not living with my father, we often checked on him. I could tell his consumption of alcohol continued. I did my best to keep plugging away and molding my future. It was what I had to do.

One morning, I called my father from work; he was working part-time at the church as a bookkeeper. Something was not right in his voice, and he was not making sense to me. I hung up and called the church secretary. She was so alarmed by his condition that she insisted on contacting an ambulance; my father was having a stroke. I immediately left the office and drove to meet my sister Kathleen at the Hospital. The drive seemed to take forever, although it was only 20 minutes from where I worked. The images of my Mom flashed in my mind and I was not ready to lose my Father.

In my mind, I was hoping this was a sign to him that his drinking had to stop. And it did.

For several months, while he recuperated, my father moved into my sister's home. He never moved back into the childhood home that had caused him so much pain after my mother passed away. After a while, he went into an assisted living facility. We actually saw a spark in his eye; he seemed happy again. This was new to him, and he needed a change away from highballs with a beer chaser. Maybe my prayers were answered, although I had no intention of going back to Sit, Stand, and Kneel. Let's chalk this one up to a guardian angel named Dolores. Thank you, Mom.

My father and I spent Saturdays either grocery shopping or visiting for a few hours, talking. I could finally talk to Dad as an adult, share my good times and bad times as well as talk about my job. I finally connected to the man I aspired to be when I was young. I told him about my life with Kyle and was able to be very open and honest. I remember sitting for hours and talking about my marriage and how he and my mother knew I was making a mistake but did not want to interfere and stop it. This was a good discussion for me, and everything was finally connecting.

Dad was an auditor and had a lot of business experience. He traveled the world and was my mentor. I wanted to be like him; he had so many connections. This was what I wanted to learn. His advice to me was be loyal to your employer and always remain humble. The loyalty I understood, but I did not grasp being humble (someday I will).

It was February 13, Dad's birthday. I went out for lunch with Denise and then shopping at Macy's for a gift. Tonight, Kyle and I would be taking Dad's gift and a cake to celebrate. I went to the cashier and was paying for his gift when my cell phone rang. The screen showed it was my sister. When I answered the call, I could immediately tell something was not right. I remember hearing those words: "Dad passed away." Like a shock wave hitting me, I froze. It was a crushing blow, and I felt ill. My dear friend Denise grabbed my hand and held on tight. How could this happen?

I remember her asking if I wanted to see him before the funeral director came to get his body. I pushed back emotions, but in total confidence, I said no. I honestly could not do it. To me, it was not real. I had to remember him alive and being happy again.

What bothered me the most is I now had a new title as orphan. Both parents were gone, and I was truly alone in the world, without the two people who brought me into it, the same two people who molded me into the person I was and will be some day. I had to grasp the new title; it would take some time.

CHAPTER 8

Life as an Orphan

It took a long time to accept my new title as an orphan. I knew what it meant, but I could not accept that it applied to me. I struggled with that in my mind and had to find a way to deal with it. This was my new reality. I held on to the memories and cherished the time my parents were on this earth. They made a difference, and I would too.

When I closed my eyes at night, I would reflect back to my childhood and look for signs of who I would become. I searched for any moment that gave me a clue into the future. When we look in the mirror, we see our reflection, but what do others see? Do they see the same person I do? Of course, we strive to see the younger version of ourselves in the mirror; who doesn't? That person we see has to go out in the world and make a difference. I never got hung up on celebrities because each of us has the same potential. Think about it. It's what they do that makes them famous; any career can get you noticed and become a celebrity. Classroom teachers out for dinner get noticed by their students. Even managers at financial institutions have star qualities when they walk into a meeting or greet their employees. We hold those cards, and what we do with them makes us special.

Finally, I built my confidence to be my own being and face the world with a sense of accomplishment and pride. At the end of the day, I was the reflection of my parents' hard work. I am the person they created; they taught me to be the man I am. My job was to make them proud.

Being in my own skin and confident with who I am opened up opportunities. I began to learn that everyone is truly different, and we need to accept that. If we were all carbon copies of each other, the world would be boring as hell, at least for me, anyway. Meeting people became much easier, and that was due to the new influences in my life. In the past, I was protective of my inner circle and hesitated deciding who I chose to socialize with. Maybe I was afraid of being hurt or I needed to have a special connection with those individuals. In the past, I never learned to like myself and had very low self-esteem. I struggled with looking at the person in the mirror because I was lost. Sure, I had big plans and wanted to be successful, but there were hesitations.

So now comfortable in my skin, I was ready for the world. I wanted to make a difference and share my story. My plan was to sell me to the world. Okay, maybe just the East Coast for now.

The purpose of my story is to give insight on how our lives in some ways are determined by the trail we lay. Not everything is in our control, but taking control is what we do. Or at least it puts us in a position to pave the next several miles with a destination in sight. We hear over and over that our lives tell a story; it's very true, and this is mine.

When we are children, our parents write our dedication in our book of life; we start chapter 1 and begin laying the additional pages out as they seem fit. The covers of our stories should be a life celebration.

So back to my story.

Every day, I got into the normal routine of work and then home. I was never one to hang out during the week, more of a homebody. We worked so hard on our home, I wanted to enjoy it. Vacation time was earned, and we looked forward to planning our next getaway. The beach is truly my happy place.

Finally, it came time to look for investment properties as a vacation home. We looked in Rehoboth Beach, and for a while, it felt like exactly the right spot. But after thinking about it, we could never escape from cold weather in the winter. So we decided to head further south to Florida, and the next debate was east or west coast. I liked the Gulf Coast and so we began looking in Tampa; we flew down on a long weekend. Before we left, we made an offer and bought a house.

CHAPTER 9

Dreams for the Future

So those dreams as a kid were starting to come to life. Not the big picture, but a snapshot of who I wanted to be. I was never unwilling to work hard for what I wanted or to keep my head above water. In that stage of life, we all made mistakes; that's part of growing up. Our eyes get bigger than the pocketbook, but somehow we suffer through it. I never liked to talk about finances or engage in religious or political conversations; they always seem to end badly.

When I started my first job, I recall putting money into a passbook savings account. My father, as an auditor, would show me how to make the debit and credit entries into my passbook. I was thrilled to see the balance go up every payday and tried my best to never make withdrawals (if we only had financial planners as teenagers).

Reflecting back at this point, I dealt with loss, not only family members but a close friend. I made it through divorce and the same that came along with it, but surely for the best. But each loss presented a new opportunity. I never lost my spirit or desire to keep moving on. I was understanding the "work humble" more and more and eventually applied that to a situation in my life. But I was getting it.

I remember conversations with my grandparents about how they came through so many hardships in their lives. Their stories were fascinating, and I wanted to know all about their childhood. The elderly have some much to offer. We never take advantage of their wisdom. In our lives now, we don't take the time to hear those stories; we simply don't make the time. Our lives have been consumed by social media and the expectation that we should work longer than an eight-hour day. We need to slow down and take it all in. If we don't, those people who have lived through hardship and failures will be gone.

How often do we gather around a table and simply discuss our days, weeks, or future plans? Our society does not even accept a simple handwritten card. We email or text. Technically, we are communicating, but verbally, we don't express our true feelings.

I conduct one-on-one meetings with my staff, and it's obvious the millennials cannot look you in the eye. When I have those meetings, I forbid cell phones in the room. I want to talk. But the art of communication and speaking in a manner to express concerns is difficult. In one of my conversations, I had an employee ask if he could text me the questions he had. Of course I said no. I cannot imagine what the business world will look like in ten years.

At lunch one day, I left the building and walked through the park across the street. I wished I had a camera. It was obvious that the future generation was in front of me. Not one person in the park was speaking to the individual sitting next to them on a bench. Heads were down, and each person was actively texting or looking through social media on their phones.

I chuckled to myself. This picture reminded me of Sunday Mass; yes, I said it. My father would announce to the congregation to bow their heads for God's blessing, but these people were not praying. I stood in the park with total amazement, thinking that we have got to change this scene. No one spoke.

We are clearly changing as a society. It's important to step back and look at our lives through various lenses. Over the years, I began to accept and welcome change. "What was is gone and what will be, is" is how I began to deal with life, love, family, and friends.

Going to work in Pittsburgh was like a family reunion. A group of us would occupy a table in the cafeteria. Over time, people knew our family sat there from 11:45 a.m. to 12:45 p.m. (Okay, sometimes until 1. Who's counting?)

We solved the problems of the bank and each other's personal lives. Nothing was off-limits. It felt good to laugh and escape the reality of our

round of cleanup was an individual who repeatedly missed time but also was protected under the Family Medical Leave Act (FMLA). FMLA is for people who have situations that require them to stay home from work. This individual did not get paid when time was missed.

After months of monitoring the situation and trying to plan staffing when this person missed work, I finally was able to find a gap. After the allotted time is used, an employee has to reapply for the benefits. In most occasions, their doctor has to approve the time off. Most employees under this law are granted three to four days off each month. When the recertification was received, the previous allotted days increased by one. Looking at the paperwork, something was not right. I contact Human Resources, and we immediately started an investigation. Well, this person was forging the paperwork; it was clear once we compared the documents over time. This was grounds for immediate termination. Apparently, this individual had been doing this for a couple of years.

Managers and supervisors need to keep their eyes open. People take advantage and expect to get away with it. The hardest piece for me to digest was using a government plan to their advantage when people who truly need assistance get rejected. It's not right. Even during the termination, this person expressed no regrets. She was more concerned with making sure I mailed her personal belongings. When I packed up her desk, I found a certificate that indicated she passed an ethics test. I placed that on the top of the box. Now what did that say?

The majority of my staff is younger than me, a mix of ethnic backgrounds too. I can reflect back to that image in the park and look around at my staff and understand that the work ethic has changed over the years. Young people today are not as dedicated to their employer (not all of them, but most). When I began my career, my father preached about a good pension and saving for retirement. He never had a 401k, so those passbook savings accounts led to financial security. This generation lived paycheck to paycheck, and most of what they purchased was on credit. Their thought process is that someday, their debt will go away. Most were not driven to buy a home when they could rent and maintain their lifestyle. The sad part is, after making those monthly payments, there was no cash flow. They did not have that extra $20 to spend on a new shirt and not have monthly payments. Listen, I have been there and hated every moment of being in debt. I changed it and worked hard to better plan my expenses and save. I want to retire at sixty-five.

I hired a new member of the team, who had worked at the bank for a few years. I never knew this, but she had FMLA too. With my previous experience, I proceeded with caution. Both these individuals were young and mothers of children. The amount of time missed at work and unpaid was incredible. How did they maintain their lifestyle and afford to have children? It would make me anxious. But I had to manage through it and make sure the other staff members understood. That was more difficult. When this individual missed work, their assignments had to be reallocated to someone else.

These are difficult discussions to have, and making sure you understand the policies is important. I never made any assumptions, as it was necessary to network with our Human Resources department. My goal was to have someone at my fingertips who could lead me through these challenges.

Developing resources in an organization or in your personal life is crucial. Resources are not meant to be taken advantage of, either. There will be some time in our lives we need help. It does not matter if you are wealthy or live paycheck to paycheck. If everyone took the time and observed the people around us for one day out of 365, we surely would identify someone who could use a hand.

Chapter 10

Defend My Honor

I would categorize myself as someone who would stand behind what I believe in and fight for my feelings and beliefs when I know it makes sense. In the past, I barely would defend myself and rarely disagreed with a direction someone gave. Behind the scenes, I would stress over it or stomp away angry but would never let anyone see those emotions. In this place now, I will not take no for an answer, and I will prepare my response to defend my emotions. I have worked too hard to give up.

In the middle of writing this book, a tragedy happened and impacted close friends. Their son died of a horrible death, one that no parent is ever prepared to accept. This young man was named Dalton, and he would light up a room with his smile. We had the pleasure to know him and will always remember his warm heart. Dalton was a special young man who was given the opportunity to have a second chance in life when he was adopted.

Our lives are fragile; how quickly things change. We don't appreciate what we have, and when tragedies happen, we find ourselves telling others how we need to live every day to its fullest. How many of us really do? We walk away from those situations and continue as if nothing has ever happened. Do we ever reflect back to the parents, children, grandparents, and anyone else in these situations and simply check in to see how they are doing? We go through the emotions of those long funeral days and never look back. Like with my father, the people who preached about keeping an eye on him never did. They forgot about it.

Early on, we are taught about life and the life cycle. I struggle to fully accept loss, but I embrace the treasure of knowing someone. In some form, they taught me something.

My advice is put the phone down during dinner, in the car, on a plane, and do one simple thing: talk.

We can apply the same concepts in business too. Our interactions with each other should not be limited to email or Skype messaging. We utilize work-from-home more and more, but I would think being at home every day would weigh on you. The only interaction with a human is your spouse, partner, or next-door neighbor, who don't always understand your job; they can't always offer support.

I have always tried to find what makes a person tick, their interests, likes, or what do they do after five o'clock. Maybe you don't want to know. We know people are different, and that should be exciting. At some point in time, there are disagreements or feelings hurt over a problem that at the end of the day is not a big deal. Simply, some of us need to be put in check.

People who hide behind lies will never be at rest. The energy it takes to keep that all together is overwhelming. Some things are sacred, and we all have secrets that we will go to our grave with, but when those lies involve others, it becomes selfish.

Jealousy gets you nowhere, as we have heard over and over. Sibling jealousy is even more difficult to accept. No matter what, we should be happy for each other; our successes are to be shared. No matter what events take place to celebrate a success, it truly is your turn to shine. You get recognized for your participation and showing that you are supportive.

Emoticons to express our likes, loves, hurts, and expressions of appreciation don't tell the whole story. Those methods are a simple way out of a conversation. We all do it, and I am guilty too. We all deserve a spoken "thank you" or "I love you" or maybe the simplest action of all, "I was thinking of you today." Those simple actionable phrases can make a difference in anyone's life.

Personally, I like to write notes for Kyle and hide them in mysterious places. I leave them in the kitchen cabinet where the coffee mugs are stored. They say, "Good morning," or "Enjoy your coffee today." I also have been known to leave a "love you" under a pillow. No matter where or when, it brings a smile. Try it.

These simple tasks hold true in business and the people we manage (or just pass in the hallway every day). Acknowledging someone means so much. Pick your head up and say, "Hello" or "Good morning" or "Thanks for coming in today." I make an effort every day to smile at a stranger walking past me in the hallway. In the morning, I walk through my department and greet each person and even compliment them on what a great job they did the previous day. If the greeting is not returned, I am okay with that, because I know it was me who made the effort.

One day recently, one of my staff did not come to work; the odd thing was she never called me to say she was taking a sick day. Not the normal behavior. I asked around to see if anyone had heard from this individual, but no one did. I began to worry and began my search to find contact information in our database. Her father was listed as her emergency contact, so I called his cell number. When he answered, I explained who I was and said that I was worried about his daughter. There was a brief pause, and he then proceeded to explain his daughter was ill. But not an upset stomach. This was serious. She tried to commit suicide. My heart sank; I was speechless. How could this be? In a matter of months, two young adults took this path. I struggle to understand suicide and the pain it causes family and friends who are left to understand why.

What drives a young adult to be so depressed that the only way out is to leave behind those who love them? It's difficult for me to understand suicide, and if I could do anything in this world, I'd want to help any way I can. Peer pressure can be so strong, and toxic people in your life can have an impact on your well-being. Stay strong, even in a world that has become so negative. We need each other.

In our jobs, there is nothing that cannot be fixed. People rush to conclusions and point blame when it's not necessary. During these stressful situations, we forget to be respectful of each other. Unless someone involved physically impacted a situation, the people helping to fix it need support from the entire team, including the leaders.

Shortly after taking my current job, I had the pleasure of dealing with an irate customer. He often yelled at me over the phone, and one day, he told me when he hears my voice, it's like, "Blah blah blah." That was enough for me. I immediately took control of the situation and addressed his unprofessional approach. I told him until he could speak to me with the same respect I give him, we would not continue our conversation.

Chapter 11

Happiness

For many years, I struggled to find my true self. Earlier in my life, I can honestly say I was not happy, maybe due to my self-esteem or because I never could find someone I had things in common with. Many years, I wondered when that empty feeling inside would end. There was a void that I had to fill. Growing up with the strict Sit, Stand, and Kneel events made it even more difficult. I had to be the image of what my religion taught me. Or did I? At some point, it was clear to me I had to figure it all out for myself. We all hear "It's a choice, and you don't have to live like that," or the best was "The Catholic church does not accept you." At that point, I said, "Bull."

I finally found myself. I was in the best relationship of my life too. We had an outstanding group of friends who saw us for who we were, in the sense of our personalities, and didn't judge by sexuality. Why is it we never judge a straight person for being straight? Oh, that is what should be normal.

Early on, I mentioned Kyle; he is the man I share my life with, an incredible man who has helped me get stronger with myself and defend what I believe. At fifty-four years old, opinions of others don't matter when it comes to my life choices. It's mine and ours. I have never been happier, and no one will change that.

In our society, our relationship is more acceptable than ever before. My company respects me too. Moving into a new neighborhood finally feels right. Even the communities we live in at our Florida properties welcome us. I don't come across feminine, nor do I wear evening gowns at night.

Those stereotypes are hopefully behind us, although they do seem to crop up once in a while.

It feels good to get a lot off my chest. Writing this book is giving me an overall sense of relief. For many years, I held so much inside, and now is the time to release what had haunted me since a young adult. Why did it take so long? The simple answer is Sit, Stand, and Kneel.

Managing people from all walks of life is fulfilling to me in so many ways. If you take out the daily complaints and "he said, she said," we all want to be respected. The people we work with truly become like family: that crazy aunt who says whatever comes out of her mouth or the cousin who makes up stories. In our work lives, we all know who those people are, and trust me, I have had them all. But in some crazy way, I would not change anything. I joke with my boss every day and say that I need to move on; he grabs his heart and tells me that he could not do it without me. I think that is his way of making me feel guilty. I do appreciate the confidence he and my staff have in me.

One person on my team does tug at my heart. Boy, is she rough around the edges too. I would do anything I could for her because I honestly have total respect. She's a single mom with two kids and doing the best she can to keep her head above water. Every couple months, she and I have our "come to Jesus" meeting. Tears are shed, but at the end of those discussions, she always says to me, "Let's hug it out." I love that. Those simple words create the biggest lump in my throat. With her, I know we can be candid and honest, and we say what we feel. There is no hiding behind smoked mirrors; it's all on the table. I like that.

As I stood in line at the Funeral Home making my way to share my condolences, I was greeted with photos of a young man with a promising future ahead of him, I began to wonder what drove us to this point. Why would Dalton orchestrate such a gathering after his life ended? The people in the line with me and who filled the Funeral Home clearly loved him. Dalton's parents are now left with unforgettable heartache? At some point, I began to get angry for his selfish act. After I went into the next room, I could hear his parents thanking everyone for their support. The words in the background just became noise, mumbled sounds. I became lost in the images of this act of no return being played over and over in my mind. My next image was Dalton's body, lying in peace. So hard to understand.

My mind was racing, and I held back tears. You know, men are tough. I wasn't. As I held the hand of this young man's mother, his father gave me a hug and held on. My anger changed for a moment because now it was the parents who need us. They are left with a process to heal with no explanation of why. And I don't have the answer they are looking for. But who does? I will always remember Dalton and will hold a spot in my heart for him. His picture hangs on my desk at work and I read the prayer on the back of his prayer card daily. Maybe it is my way to speak with him and not let his memory be forgotten.

When someone passes away from illness or old age, it's sad, but we accept it. It's the life cycle. Illness is sometimes hard to let go but for whatever reason, we accept the outcome. We try to prepare ourselves enough for the end. Some people plan their funeral and final arrangements. I used to think that was strange.

One of our good friends plans to have the ashes of her pets buried with her. I can accept that. I joke that I want her jewelry. But I respect that she has planned so far ahead. For me, I want nothing. No service; no Sit, Stand, and Kneel. Just be done. Off to the next life.

The things we make so difficult in our daily jobs seem pointless after dealing with day-to-day life and tragic events like the loss of loved ones. We devote so much time explaining ourselves when issues arise and sometimes individuals tend to push for explanations that are pointless. Onetime events turn into a novel of pointless explanations that become a grouping of words in an email. These acts of understanding a mistake costs countless hours and pulls people into a task of defining a root cause. The sad part is one or two people will react to the analysis, and simply put, it will never get read again.

In situations that we need to recap a customer issue, it's important to state facts and move on. Most important is to assure the customer is whole. Mindless efforts to regurgitate the issue over and over are only an act to make sure people involved understand the problem. It goes no further.

I start my day by reading countless emails and to prioritize which issues require immediate attention. I do my best to put things into perspective and make a to-do list for the day. I keep a notepad beside my laptop at work. Throughout the day, I scratch items off as I respond to these emails. I find myself laughing at the endless "Reply all" messages that fill up my mailbox. If only people would take a moment to call. Those emails do not make the issue get resolved any sooner; they cause more confusion in the end because each person on that "To:" line thinks someone else is handling it.

Every day, from the minute we open our eyes, we make choices. We choose to hit snooze or accept that the alarm went off and get out of bed to start a new day. It's interesting to think about yesterday and how many choices we made throughout the day. I bet you lose track. It's truly amazing: The simple things we do require us to make a choice. As our day goes on, our decisions become more complex. What we decide could impact so many others, not like the choice to wear blue socks or black socks. Managers rely on others to take direction and make decisions for themselves. If we don't follow up on those decisions, our business could suffer a loss. I'm not one to micromanage my staff, but I do my best to keep informed of any situation that may escalate: challenging at times, and most situations are rewarding.

I began to partner with other areas of the bank; one area that's similar to mine was an opportunity for a critical partnership, even though they manage many more products. Early on, I could see opportunities for me and my staff. I immediately got on board and began to strengthen the relationship. In many businesses, you have to plan your own future and work hard to get it. As the manager of this team says, "Take over the world." Funny thing is, my fortune cookie had a similar message. Was it finally coming true?

At one point in my career path, I was an individual contributor and hated it. I actually found myself wanting to lead situations that I had to simply observe; that drove me nuts, but it was my "Ah ha" moment.

I know it's important to address potential client issues that could have substantial impact. But speculation is just that. We need to understand and take all things into consideration before we react. Not all situations require immediate attention, especially Sunday afternoon on Mother's Day. Really? It turned out to be nothing major at all. I did laugh when someone in a group text message responded saying, "No one at the company is responding." I held back, as my response would have been, "It's Sunday, Mother's Day; do you not get it?" I held my tongue.

These are situations we need to digest and handle accordingly.

Sometimes, first reactions can be the worst. Even if you think it's nonsense at the moment, you have to look at the whole picture. These are the lessons we have to make sure our staff understands too. I can think of a couple people on the team who would have reacted the same way I was thinking but did not.

It's amazing; in business, we mold ourselves into people we are normally not like outside of nine to five. We bring on a different personality at work. Did you ever wonder why? Maybe because we want to hide behind who we really are at home. I think the influences of our jobs tend to create our personalities. At home, I do not speak on the phone to irate clients; I become that client if I have an issue to address. You begin to get a sense of what it is like to be on the other end of that phone.

Every business does an internal audit on a variety of processes. One of mine is listening to our recorded lines. The customer service representatives are recorded so we can use those calls for training and to have a record of a client issue if necessary. The reps know we listen to these calls. To say I have heard it all is an understatement. I have heard personal calls with bill collectors to spouses calling to complain about whatever happened the previous night. No matter how many times I have told my staff to be careful what they talk about and of course encourage them to make personal calls on break or lunch, it never seems to sink in.

The most embarrassing call was between one of my reps and her husband. The discussion started out very loving, but the back-and-forth of "I love you," "No, I love you more" turned into the bombshell of "How many guys did you sleep with before we got married?" Then it turned very sexual. I think my face turned fifty shades of red. So now I had to address this issue with my rep. What an uncomfortable situation; how to best explain what I heard? After I finally got my words out, I was more shocked by the reaction: She had no remorse. Oh, these millennials.

Do people really think before they respond to emails or a text? What we put in writing can always come back to strike. I reread my messages and make sure my distribution list is correct or the person I am responding to is the only individual on the "To:" line. Sure, there are times you have to soften the reply after reading what your emotions tell you to type. Our fingers type the words our heads are truly saying, but the other side of the brain that controls my actions puts the brakes on and says, "Hold up, brother." Glad that side takes control sometimes.

I had an employee send an instant message to a coworker, which is not a problem at all; it occurs multiple times a day. In the middle of the back-and-forth conversation, a client issue arose, and this individual began chatting with a more seasoned salesperson. The salesperson is exceptional but also can be demanding. Knowing her, I have no issues with that and respect the position. My employee was not paying attention and instead of responding to her coworker, she sent an emoticon demonstrating frustration. That would have been okay, but this person proceeded to express her frustration toward the salesperson, again thinking it was a coworker.

This is a good example of making sure you don't respond with emotion and reread before hitting Send. So the fireworks began, and I jumped in to ease the situation. True to form, my rep called me at home to alert me of the situation; I respected that. She knew it was wrong and prepared herself for the consequences.

The next morning, I began to smooth the event over and immediately contacted the salesperson. After hearing the frustration and disappointment in her voice, I could only express my overall dissatisfaction for the events that took place. I reassured her I would speak to the rep and certainly would address it according to Human Resource policies.

It's amazing what we can accomplish by speaking one-on-one. The tone of someone's voice or visible body language reveals so much. As complex human beings, we need these clues. You don't get that in a text. Just like when you meet someone for the first time, that initial impression is so important. The impression you make is important too. I am a big believer in the saying "Dress for success," especially for a job interview. Eye contact is equally effective and proves you are sincere and holds the attention of the individual you are speaking to. These are simple expressions that seem to be disappearing today.

CHAPTER 12

Job Openings

It's always interesting to interview new candidates for a position at the bank. I could write a book on those experiences and the dos and don'ts. The new generation obviously suffers from the me syndrome. Back in the day, I was taught to send a thank you note after someone interviewed me; it was common courtesy and demonstrated respect. In today's world, I would also accept an email, but clearly, this does not always happen. And how you dress for an interview shows respect (or not). I recently interviewed a young man who was wearing jeans and a golf shirt. Before the questions began, he made me aware that he was just chilling at his parents' home for the summer and was in no rush to get a job. He had been laid off and was collecting Unemployment and wanted to ride that out for a bit. If I were rude, I could have ended the conversation and ask him to leave. I did not and wanted to hear his full story. In some ways, I was intrigued, especially since occurred while I his writing this book.

This young man had a college education and was not sure what direction he was going. None of his past jobs were related to his education. He commented that his parents forced him to get a degree. I asked why. The next response did not shock me; I hear it over and over. Family history included a college education, and that is what the expectation was for this young man.

This new generation makes me a bit nervous. I often wonder what will become of our world. At times, I feel afraid to venture out in the world to find new opportunities; trust me, I am not looking at this point. I want to be able to reach out to whoever I can and help prepare them for what is going to be. Our society has lost the simple task of communication in a verbal form; we don't even teach our children to handwrite a letter.

Trying to find employment is difficult these days and a challenge for anyone looking. There is so much competition out there, and selling yourself has never been so important. Many organizations are not aggressive enough with poor performance; I'm certainly not proposing we terminate people who are not doing well, but we need to dig both feet in the ground and work hard to improve the current situation. Our society has become fixed on preventing lawsuits, which have become a common practice in all industries. In the end, people are responsible for their own outcomes and need to take ownership for themselves. In most cases, the company was not at fault; it's the employee who failed to perform. What a shame.

As kids, we listened to our parents and grandparents tell stories about their childhoods. They taught us about their struggles and how they overcame it. These days, there are very few conversations around the Sunday dinner table at Grandma's.

It's funny that in order to stay in touch with family, we refer to Facebook. Sure, there are family picnics, holiday dinners, and the occasional "Hey, we haven't seen you in a while; let's get together." We have become more wrapped up in our own inner circles that we neglect to recognize our upbringings and those memories of family.

I actually want to establish a cell phone basket in our home. Anyone coming in the front door has to leave their phone in the basket. We want to visit with you, not your friends on Facebook, Instagram, or Snapchat. I'm guilty to doing Facebook check-ins; it's fun at the time, but as I began thinking about it, I started to get nervous. The bottom line is, you are letting all two hundred friends know you are not home, and your home is vacant. So their friends and friends of theirs can eventually know where you are. Some of those apps even track your exact location. The sad part is friendships have been hurt by social media. Be cautious and know your audience. That's my advice.

The old saying that "Life changes within an instant" is so very true. When you think your day-to-day tasks become routine or even predictable, things happen that cause you to regroup and take assessment of your surroundings. That includes work life too (actually, we spend more time at work these days than at home; it's sort of a sad thought, but it is reality).

Every organization eventually makes changes; one day, you report to one department, and the next day, you are an individual contributor. I used to wonder if the people making these changes really understand the business. In some organizations, I'm not so sure. Our lives take the same path.

One day, life is good, and we look forward to the next day; others hit with a blow that sends us spinning. I am guilty of public display of emotions, frustrations, or roadblocks on social media. The occasional daily thought or the extended reach for support from our friends is gratifying. But do those friends truly come to your aid? Of course, they click "like" but can you think of a time when one of those people actually contacted you? I watch friends post personal stories and pictures from their hospital room; first of all, that certainly is too much information. I always tell my staff to reread before you write something that you don't want to come back and bite you in the ass.

We no longer have privacy in our lives and continue to fall into that realm of social media. The bottom line is, we do have control and need to take charge of what we want others to see. If we don't utilize the tools to control our privacy settings, then that's on us.

The same holds true in our jobs. Sometimes, just saying nothing is a good thing. There should be a limit of what you share with your staff; they don't need to know who you sleep with or what you and your life partner argued about. Opening up that door can lead to people taking advantage of you. They find your weakness and know how to push your buttons.

We all have a voice that needs to be heard. I do; it's a good one too. Funny. I attribute my newfound voice to Kyle; honestly, he taught me to say no and express how I feel in various situations. That might be why I have high blood pressure: For so many years, I was silent. For the most part, I am generally a laid-back kind of guy, a calming personality. I am like that at work. Clients could be screaming at me over the phone, and I tend to smooth out the situation. My staff knows when I have had enough when they hear me say my key word: "Really." They laugh when they hear me say that, and the tone of my voice becomes very pronounced. What's your key word? Think about it.

So no matter the situation, life changes by the minute. Some changes we can control; others are not that easy. Life events lay the roadmap to our future; they certainly tell our story. If we can only capture everything

C H A P T E R 1 3

Acts of Kindness

Acts of kindness go a long way, whether they are small, like a thank you, or a larger one, like a monetary gift. We tend to support the underdog; in our hearts, we get wrapped up in the tale, and our first instinct is to give. Some of us fall for these people and want to lend and hand, but others turn their backs. Either is okay; the person giving (or not) has to feel satisfied for doing what their heart told them.

In some situations, the receiver takes advantage, and we fall for it. Every afternoon, when I drive home from work, I see a man or woman holding a "Homeless" sign at a traffic light. Recently, I began to observe how often the drivers passing by stopped and gave gifts of money for these individuals. I fell for it too. So I really began to watch and study the people standing at the light. Each has a unique presence, and with a closer look, I made some interesting observations.

The woman had a manicure, her hair was trimmed, washed, and styled. Her clothing was not torn or dirty, and her eyewear was stylish. You may think I'm crazy, but I study these people every day. A man sometimes takes the woman's place; he has a trimmed goatee, his hair was recently cut, and his sneakers are more stylish than mine. After studying them for a month or so, I finally stopped giving. I don't want to judge, but my observations made me skeptical.

These individuals made a life choice at some point that brought them to this place. Yes, I feel sad for them, but my sorrow is more because of their deceit.

So I really have become more observant in my job and other situations.

I may be a silent listener, but I tend to take it all in before I comment or make a move that changes the direction of my team.

I never took the phrase "What goes around, comes around" seriously, but I am a firm believer now. The mistakes we make come back to us, in some form. It's not always the best situation, but it should make us think. When we are dealt with a tragedy, we look to blame others or beat ourselves up (asking, "Why me?").

Some things are out of our control, especially the death of a loved one. It's hard to understand why it happened, so we tend to think of how I could have loved that person more, or what actions did I take to bring me these feelings of guilt? If you hurt someone by inappropriate actions, it was wrong to begin with; the guilty feeling we have should direct us to reflect on our past actions and determine what led us there to begin with. As human beings, feelings of guilt can be hard to manage. We learned to feel this way while grow up.

Every one of us wants to feel loved and have the security of a positive relationship. If you don't have that or are sad about where your life is going, then work on changing it if you can. Take charge.

Each of us has the need to help someone less fortunate. At any point, we all could use a helping hand, whether in times of sorrow or in celebration. We acknowledge accomplishments and praise those who go above and beyond. It's important for people to feel good about something they did with a positive result. But those negative situations can be turned into an advantage. Certainly address an error or discuss why someone's handling of an issue did not meet your expectations. But thank that person for trying. How would they have learned right from wrong? It bothers me when a manager yells at an employee in front of their staff. Their mistake could be a result of your own error. Did you train them correctly and give them the appropriate tools they need? Step back and think before you address it, and do so in private.

There are often times when people make mistakes that impact a client. I have dealt with many of those situations. My approach is to document every conversation you have with an individual. You may never need those notes, but at least you have them in your back pocket.

I conduct one-on-one meetings with my staff each month. We talk about errors, work volume, and anything they feel is necessary. I make direct eye contact with each person and expect the same; when someone isn't telling me the truth and is just telling me what I want to hear, I can sense their body language change. Funny how uncomfortable people are with looking you in the eye. What are they hiding? My grandmother always told me that eye contact is the most important type of communication; it's the path to someone's soul.

Kids are the best because they say whatever comes to their minds: no filter. As they mature, the filter becomes defined by the adults who influence them. So as they move into adulthood, personalities become clearer but are driven by others. Early on, we are molded into the person we become. As I watched my aunt age, her filter reverted somewhat back to childhood (or she is just more relaxed). So many questions about aging and how we position ourselves for the future. Other people do influence us in a positive and negative way; nothing wrong with that, and a healthy mix is good.

I tend to do a lot of soul-searching when I have alone time. I tend to think of the past, my family, and those memories that last a lifetime. I play those special moments over and over in my mind; I capture each conversation and expression that brought a smile to my face. Sometimes, I imagine a different outcome. Of course, I cannot change the past, but remembering it is so important.

I wish I could capture the special moments of my childhood that brought me so much joy. There were many, and when I look back, family was most important. Our inner circle of cousins were very close; we grew up together. In our adult years, we separated as our lives went in different directions, as life should, and now that inner circle is coming back around. It's interesting to see, after fifty-four years, how the life cycle occurs.

CHAPTER 14

Job Description

In my job, I am on the phone all day (well, most of the day). Of course, that would fit, managing a customer service department. I try to resolve issues; my customers feel as though their issue was addressed, and it won't happen again. Our role at the bank requires human intervention; we all make mistakes. So do our customers. When I am asked to document a response that supports that we won't make the same error twice, I really have to think. That is surely a loaded question.

True to form, we dig in and document a response that supports what we can promise. It sure is frustrating when a month later, the same error happens, and we have to fall on our sword and admit human error again. Customers just don't want to hear that. In this day and age, they feel we should have systemic controls in place that promise error-free work. I wish it was that simple.

From my experiences with customers, I have a new appreciation for anyone working in that industry, especially the service representative who answers my call when I am having cable or cell phone issues. It's highly unlikely that the individual on the other end of the phone personally caused my issue. So why should I take out my frustrations on them? The company is responsible to provide that person training and a script that will assist them in answering my questions. If these individuals struggle to resolve a problem, our next step is to speak with a manager or supervisor. Those individuals are responsible for making sure their staff is prepared.

Let's face it. The customer is not always right, and we know that. We need to make them feel they are, but truthfully, that is not the case. It's difficult to make that distinction sometimes, so the bottom line is, we need to keep the customer calm and fix the problem.

Recently, I called a client to discuss a problem we were having. It was an eye-opener because there was an immediate disconnect on what their expectations were; we did our best to explain how our process was supposed to work. That's never a comfortable conversation to have with a client, and we finally had to tell them they were wrong. So we began pulling up examples and walking them through our decision process. By the end of the meeting, the client actually agreed with our approach. It's important to do that in any situation; if you are leading the conversation, it is critical to accept criticism on both sides. It strengthens the overall relationship.

CHAPTER 15

Reflections

At some point in our lives, we need to slow down and reflect on the day-to-day. Take in the moment and understand the direction we want to take. Of course, you can never go back, but certainly you can work on the future. So many times, I would hear my parents and grandparents say how fast life passes by when you get older. As I kid, I would count down the days until a holiday or the next beach trip. Those weeks felt like years. Now a simple invite to dinner or upcoming event comes upon us so fast. How do we slow that down? We have to treasure our moments and take it all in, enjoy what has been given to us.

I recently returned from vacation and had time to think and put life into perspective. Floating in a pool helps, but it was time well spent. I thought about where I started and where I am today; at some point, I had to stop and push back my emotions. Interesting enough, I obviously made the right choices because I am truly happy. My relationship is solid, and my social life is full of people I have personally selected to be in my network. In some way, each of those people have touched my life, which had meaning. Some closer than others, but that is normal. The emotions arise when you think about our losses; again, we can never reverse that. It's the life cycle.

As we age, there seems to be a new reality of me time: time to enjoy life and friends, laugh, and live. Do we only accept that in our adulthood and not as children? Even though we spend time with our childhood friends, pretending and talking about our dreams, it's interesting to observe children talking about their futures. We used to live for the moment and fly by the seat of our pant. When did we lose that concept? When we take on more responsibility in our adult lives, we become planners and begin to lay down our goals. Those plans change along the way, but we do our best to stay focused on long-term goals.

When I look back at friends and family who have gone to college and pursued a degree they hoped would give them fulfillment, I chuckle. In so many instances, those same people are doing nothing related to their college education. The endless classes that are prerequisites to a piece of paper we hang on a wall become a thing of the past. Who uses calculus now? To get a business degree, I had to take a chemistry class. I surely am not mixing the next moisturizer cream at my desk. My sister spent five grueling years obtaining a pharmacy degree; she now owns a store that sells dance school fitness wear. Do colleges spend time truly thinking about the outcomes of education and ensuring students are gaining knowledge? I doubt it.

When I think about education beyond high school, I worry that we force our young people into a college education. First, most are not ready, and second, we are losing the arts of craftsmanship in our world. If a young adult expresses interest in becoming a plumber, builder, or artisan, we need to encourage it. That piece of paper hanging in an office or shoved in a box under your bed does not necessarily mean you are prepared for all situations that come your way.

I have done a lot of hiring over my career and am fascinated by the backgrounds of some candidates. It's amazing to see people who take a total direction change; they start out as a nurse and are now a banker. They go from architect to selling floral arrangements at the local grocery store. How do you ever predict what you will eventually become? You don't; you can't.

I have had multiple positions throughout my working life, but they were all related. But since joining the banking community, I have basically stayed in treasury services, payment processing, or lockbox services. I did once hold the position of a chicken at the mall. Oh, how our lives change and evolve.

I love life, I love people, and I love entertaining. It's a rush for me to plan a dinner party and have everything set. Sometimes I overthink things, but the end result always seems to work nicely. If there is one compulsion I have (and yes, Kyle would agree), I enjoying cleaning. It's my obsession to spend my Saturday morning cleaning. My satisfaction is knowing the house is clean and ready for company at any time. Even when we travel to our home in Florida, I make sure upon leaving the house is spotless for our next visit. I apply that same obsession to managing staff. I plan, act, and make sure my team performs well, especially to prepare for the next client issue. It's discipline. We learn that early on when our parents set rules for us to follow. For me, I always tried to understand why I was wrong and worked to better myself. I would defend my actions if I felt strongly that I was not wrong. I do that today. Sometimes, we hide behind our wrong and blame someone else; it's easier for us to get the heat off and watch the other person fail. I cannot understand why anyone would get a rush from seeing someone else fail. I think it comes down to jealousy.

We need many people to make our lives work. I need my manager, who needs me to manage my staff. My employees need our customers so they can live their lives, and I need my staff to grow our business so that helps all of us earn more money. It all makes sense; we rely on so many people every day. If one of those people are out for the day, it impacts the chain. The missing link.

That's why I preach to my staff about their attendance and how missing a day impacts the team. It's amazing how one person can change the events for the day.

I don't know when life changed to the point we don't take in the moments of the day or even appreciate our surroundings. It's makes me sad when I see young people on the beach, facing the Gulf of Mexico, and none of them really see the view in front of them. They are addicted to electronic devices, which have become the most unwelcome visitor in our existence. Instead of seeing what our world has to offer, we tweet, text, or post our location for everyone else to see.

For our world to exist, we need to return to some of the old ways of doing things. I have said this before, but the art of communication is lost.

In my job, I always follow the "sundown rule": Basically, the rule is, you respond to all emails the same day you receive them, before sundown (that includes voice messages too). You may not have the entire answer, but acknowledging the customer is essential. It also shows respect for their business.

Separation of Duties

W ork life and personal life are valuable in so many ways. We need to work, but we also need our downtime. But even our downtime can take time away from our relaxation, and that's okay to some degree. When you accept the responsibilities as a manager, the role does come with an expectation that when a situation arises, you will step up.

When I go away, my laptop is always with me. I'm not saying it's for everyone, but I stay connected as much as possible. Maybe it's because I want to keep a pulse on the business, but most important, I want to know what's happening while I'm gone. I have worked too hard to let things slip. I know I cannot control everything, and I don't want to, because mistakes will be made, and we need those mishaps to learn.

If we manage the people who work for us to handle things in our absence, then it's their job to step up and handle a problem. We often have career development conversations with our staff; it's during those meetings we begin to mold our key players. You want to surround yourself with people who will be able to handle anything that may arise.

Developing future leaders in our organizations is rewarding. There is no guarantee for any of us in corporate America. Every day is different, and we need to accept the challenges that face us and work hard. In so many situations, it's key to own your destiny and make sure you earn the respect of others. We always hear that you never know who your boss will be some day. I have seen that happen for the good and bad. So the saying of "Put on a happy face" comes to mind, or "Never let them see you sweat." You know for yourself when it is time to pursue other career opportunities.

Every organization goes through changes, including personnel changes. Most times, it is for the better of the business; some changes are temporary until a more suitable solution is found. But even those temporary changes can lead to a lot of questions. I find it awkward to make a staffing change unless I understand the background. Regardless if you are impacted or not, I think opinions matter, especially if you can identify potential issues. That could vary, but if the business could be at risk, then everyone has to weigh in.

It's good to have people you can turn to for their opinion. Many individuals give valuable input and make it seem more acceptable. Never give a knee-jerk reaction, even if you don't agree. Play the game and ride it out. If it turns out to be a bad choice, then put your feelers out and begin contacting your network. We all want to succeed and have goals for our careers. If you don't, I highly recommend it.

When you meet with your manager, take notes and come with your own agenda. Make sure you discuss each item you have listed. If possible, send your manager the list ahead of your meeting. That gives your manager time to digest what the conversation will be.

Sure, these are all things we should be doing, but you have to find your own way of communicating your intentions.

CHAPTER 17

Influences in Our Lives

When you think about the friends you have and the neighbors you interact with regularly, do you ever try to figure out what the connections are? In some way, those individuals have something in common, and you have invited them into your inner circle. Through our childhood and business interactions, we bring people in who will be good mentors.

We fill the gaps in our inner circles with people who have influenced us over the years, even at a young age. Think about it. Someone is the mothering figure, another is a father figure, and others share the traits of your best friend from childhood. Their personalities are similar, and we turn to those people for support in time of need. Or just a twenty-minute phone conversation to catch up. As we age, it's true that we revert back to our childhood in some form.

My Aunt Collette is ninety-four and lives in a nursing home. In her prime, she was a bank teller and worked in a local department store. She had a remarkable life, with the exception of not having children of her own. With my own family being so close, we adopted her when our mother passed away so young. She had to be the rock.

Aunt Collette was a dependable babysitter for our family. I remember going to her house and making tents out of bed comforters and dining room chairs in the living room. We had so much fun. My favorite memory is when my Aunt Collette sang to me before bedtime. She thought she sounded like Barbra Streisand, but I remember turning toward her and saying, "Don't sing." She would always laugh, and we talked about that for many years.

Now that she's in her nineties, that personality no longer exists. It is sad to me when I visit her now; I don't know if she realizes who I am. We joke about her age, and when I say she is ninety-four, her response is, "That cannot be." Our conversations don't really last long, and we often to talk about the past. She was a teller for the same bank I work for now. That's funny. For many years, I would hear the story of how her stocks split; she had six hundred shares. The sad aspect was those shares were used to pay for her care.

I look around at the other men and woman who live in the same nursing home as my aunt. They argue with each other and don't really hold full-length conversations. It's an existence that we all fear, but the reality is, this may be us some day.

My Aunt Colette was a great role model to all of us. She lived through the loss of her parents, two sisters, and a brother. In addition, she lost her husband too. When I think back about how I felt being an orphan, I remind myself of my aunt.

This is a good example of developing your inner circle and a network of people you can count on. If it was not for our immediate family, she would have no one to visit her. There are so many days I stop and think about her, our family, and how lonely she must feel.

Early on, when we set our goals and establish family bonds, we need to remember who will be left when we are alone and trying to remember our past.

My Aunt Colette took care of so many people in her life and cherished the friendships she had. The reality is, she has outlived those same people.

Chapter 18

Fresh Start

Sometimes in our careers and personal life, we have to reinvent ourselves. Some may say it's as simple as a new hairstyle or clothing choices. That may be true, but in some instances, it should include our personalities too. That is a bit harder and not as easy for some. If we take the observations of our past and the conflicts we encounter along the way, digging deep inside can lead to a new you.

Growing up, I didn't always defend myself; normally, I would not speak up. Thinking back, I let people influence my decisions and allowed people to push me in one direction. Finally, I looked at my past and dug inside to give my personality a new look. I certainly don't allow people to intimidate me now. I am more open to express my opinions and say something when I disagree. I am more confident with me.

That's a hard place to reach because you need to be critical of yourself. It's okay, though. I think back, and those difficult experiences dealing with staff issues contributed to my change. In addition, a strong relationship has provided me with the support I need. Solid working relationships have contributed too.

Exchanging a simple smile as you walk down the hallway or sidewalk can make you and the person you're passing feel important—as long as you don't stare or trip them by mistake. You don't want to come across as a stalker!

One of my goals is to pay someone a compliment every day. You could simply tell a person they look nice today or say thank you for coming in.

One of my current employees and I always try to say how glad we are to see each other. I know it is silly, but it puts a smile on her face; me too.

But in the past, I never did that; I feel badly that I failed to recognize my surroundings. There were many times a simply thank you would have made someone's day. People work hard and we need to recognize good deeds. When we get outstanding service in a restaurant just say thank you. We all want to be acknowledge and at the end of the day did it really cost us anything? Be kind.

As I look in the past, there were many years I was truly sad. I cannot pinpoint the cause, but I know it impacted my well-being. Of course, I went through and overcame significant life events, so my sadness was more about not being happy in my teenage years. Of course, high school was horrible; thank goodness it was only four years.

Those teen years were awkward, and I found myself influenced by Sit, Stand, and Kneel. It was more like I had to live up to those expectations. I was not up for that challenge, and now looking back, I played along not to hurt others, mainly my family. Basically, I was putting on a front to make others respect me.

I understand why we do those things, but owning yourself from an early age is so important. I'm not saying to disrespect your family, but talking about your emotions should be on top of your list. I can only imagine if I had been more open about how I was feeling and asked the questions that kept filling my head.

So many families go through a divorce or separation. We tend to choose sides, and it never seems to work when you play the mutual card. That is so hard to do. It does work for some, but at some point, it won't. Your choice to support one side can be influences by the majority. Family sticks with family, right? That is what we do, and we are taught it's the right thing. I tend to agree and have done both in the past, only to end up hurt in the end. I guess it goes back to speaking your mind and being honest. If people can separate and be fair with each other, why is it that most relationships that end break up a family too?

Networking

A ny relationship goes through turmoil at some point. It happens in our personal lives and in business. In some ways, I think it is a test of how strong we are and our abilities to adapt. You can never predict it; the initial shock tends to leave us with negativity, but only until you digest the situation and plan your own direction. This is a good opportunity to develop your own plan and take control. In some situations, it leads to a positive outcome.

If I relate this to a business situation, I can equate it to a change in management. Our bank recently had a reorganization, and I now report to someone else. I was okay with that, and the concept of renewing my career was an inspiration. So I took matters into my own hands and began networking within our organization, making sure my name did not go unnoticed. I was ready for more and want to be sure others knew that too. It's encouraging and rewarding to sell yourself to someone who doesn't know you. It also proves that you have ambition and would welcome a helping hand.

One week, I began to look at the overall picture. I had to decide my next move and do what was best for me and my career. Repeatedly, I mention building a network of people who you can turn to and get advice from, so that is exactly what I did. I made more contacts and looked at opportunities that fit my career goals. That's what you have to do.

In so many situations, you need to design your path and coordinate the execution of where you want to be in ten years. I always hated that question during job interviews: "Where do you see yourself in ten years?" It's a loaded question.

When you have those yearly goal-setting conversations with your manager, it is the perfect time to discuss your career path, but make sure he or she listens and hold them accountable to help you get there. Most managers agree, notate the discussion, but never execute the plan you propose.

So after a few sleepless nights, I put on my happy face and accepted the changes. In some ways, I felt strongly that this was only to be temporary. That helped me digest it a bit more. I don't hold grudges, but I expect a lot from others. If I work hard and am dedicated to my work, the person I report to should be the same as a leader.

I used to joke with my prior boss, "It was the Becker way, so get on board." I even bought him a T-shirt with "Team Becker" on it.

Even in our jobs, we have to laugh.

So once the dust settles and we take inventory of ourselves and the team it's back to business as normal. At the end of the day, we cannot impact our clients with the disruptions that we tend to hold heavy on our shoulders. In some way or another, everything tends to work out for the best. But never let your guard down and remain positive. It's okay to worry about change because it shows you truly have an emotional attachment to what you do. Your passion to be successful is what matters most to you.

Keep the conversations going and don't hesitate to express your opinions, while remaining professional, of course.

CHAPTER 20

Setting Your Goals

When you identify an opportunity, the best course of action is to pursue it. Set a goal and go after what you want. It's not just to gain financial security each time but also to earn respect and gain a reputation that stays with you. Most people tend to sit back and wait for something to happen.

Never step on anyone's toes when trying to reach your ultimate goal; there are times it's appropriate to utilize the next level of your organizational chart. Nothing wrong with that. I recommend you never bad-mouth anyone in the same organization, so the conversation needs to be about what you want to accomplish. Get your thoughts together and make notes for yourself. It's like buying a new car. You know what options you want, the color, and the model. So go after it.

When I was applying for a job, I always researched who the hiring manager was and took time to send a note letting them know I applied for a job within their department. My message also included a brief summary of my prior work and how I could lend value to the team (almost like placing an ad in the newspaper; you want to give as much information in a few words).

An interview should be interactive and the conversation seamless. It does not always need to be about answering silly questions of "Where do you see yourself in ten years', "Tell me about a time when ...," "If you did X and Y happened, how would you react?" I get the purpose of those questions, but a conversation about the person's resume usually reveals so much about them.

Generally, I always lead off with a description about the job opening and what "a day in the life of ..." is like for the person in the position. I want to hear the person I am meeting with speak and tell me how they are the best candidate, and I want to learn more about them. Anyone can learn new functions, but at the end of the day, his or her personality is key. I could hire a professor who has three degrees, include an MBA. To me, that matters less than the right attitude.

If I have to meet with this same person in the future because their performance is less than standard, I want to know how they will react. In that situation, the degrees are useless.

I never judged anyone on the level of degree they held because I feel strongly that other factors weigh into an employee's ability to perform the job. It comes down to common sense and on-the-job experience.

It's good to keep the interview conversation away from personal issues. Some people try to share their family stories and equate them to the job opening or tie them together with the job requirements. I have been on interviews that last hours and some that take thirty minutes. I have mixed feelings on both, so I would say use your judgment.

Oh, and I am not in favor of multiple interviews for one position. Get everyone together at one time, and don't have a candidate inconvenienced with multiple meetings. That's just common sense.

CHAPTER 21

Dream Big

often dream about the future and fantasize about where I will be and what will my life become. I tend to think the worst, but lately, I have become more optimistic. Really think: It goes back to how you feel overall, and that sets the stage for your dreams. Of course, having a bad day can lead to dreams of people chasing you or being naked in a public place. Yes, I have had those types of dreams. One time, I dreamt I was in a conference room for a meeting, and I was the only one naked. Good Lord.

When I have a good day or good thoughts about my future, I see myself being successful and surrounded by people who are influential in our community. I dream of cocktail parties and driving up to my mansion in my Maserati. Okay, so I think bigger than my pocketbook. It's fun to have an escape.

Our moods dictate a lot about how we feel, and stress does a number on our beings. We tend to have pains we did not have before and sometimes a headache that never seems to leave us. When I am stressed, I lose weight because I have no appetite. That's the total opposite of others, but that is how my body reacts.

About eight years ago, I went through the lowest point of my life. I truly thought I would never pull through. It was the low of lows.

At several points during that time, I would have emotional breakdowns and found it hard to pull myself up and move on. But somehow I did; it was not easy, but I had to.

I had nightmares during this horrible time, and I could not shake them off. I remember waking up in cold sweats and thinking my world was about to crash.

I had to find me inside and take control. My partner, sister, brother-in-law, and friends were by my side, and I did not want to let them down. So I dug in and took control of my depression.

I started to set goals for myself and had to see those through. I began taking notes and keeping a log of my accomplishments each day. I would write down what I had to complete each day and week, and doing that gave me the inner strength to keep going. Honestly, it took months to come back, but it was a truly humbling experience that I will remember for my lifetime.

It was interesting to see who supported me at that time and who kept their distance. I don't have any negative feelings for those people who chose to stand back, but I have the outmost love and respect for those who held me up.

I don't think people really know how to react; maybe for them, it's more difficult to get involved. Never stand back because people need each other. I have shared personal loss and expressed how much we need each other.

It's never easy to admit your failures or say that you need help. It's important to always be positive because situations change, and you have the control to improve the outcome. When you are in that situation, you don't feel like you can climb out of that hole, but you will, and as a better person.

Take a deep breath and turn to your inner thoughts and dig into those long-term goals and childhood conversations. The answer may be there somewhere.

What Was Is Not What Is Today

One of the lost arts in our new society is the simple expression of sending a card or note giving thanks, congratulations, or thinking about you. It's easy to compose an email or a text with a smiley face at the end. We are about to lose the art of a handwritten note. Most schools are no longer teaching cursive writing. To me, that is extremely sad.

There was always mystery in analyzing someone's handwriting. I remember hearing that having open symbols meant you were creative. Things like that were interesting to me. Some fortune-tellers relied on handwriting to analyze your future.

Email has become the preferred means of communication, even when corresponding with clients. Some people use all capital letters to make sure the receiver gets it, but that can be taken as yelling.

I think in certain situations, a phone call is more feasible. Hearing someone's voice can be more calming, unless the person on the other end insists on being rude. We have all experienced those types of calls. It's better to get control and try to smooth out the conversation.

How will our future executives communicate with each other? Technology will lead the way and dictate how we can deliver our messages most effectively. There are some practices that are not so bad. Think about the people who are designing these new means of communication. They are our young generation who have no experience with using a rotary phone or sending a letter. I bet they don't even know how to address an envelope.

In restaurants now, there are devices at each table to order your food and even pay for it. Eventually, you won't need a waitress (maybe just to deliver your food). Grocery stores have implemented self-checkout lanes and eliminated the need for a clerk to ring up your order.

I am guilty too. I cannot remember the last time I went into a bank branch and spoke to a teller; I always use the automated teller machine. It's easy, and you can conduct most banking transactions without seeing a person.

Human intervention is going extinct. I appreciate going to the theater and seeing people perform. I rarely go to see a movie, and the last time I did, that was automated too. You buy your tickets on-line and pick them up at a kiosk. I can accept most of what our world is offering, but in some way, I am holding out on keeping those old ways.

But we have to remain competitive and outdo the next guy. If we don't, then we would have nothing new to offer.

In any situation, it's about competition and being on the winning team, whether you are inventing the newest technology or simply implementing improvements in your workplace.

So many companies utilize outside firms to help develop process improvements and gain efficiencies. Many of those programs fizzle out after time. They never last, even after so much money is spent. They force people to rethink what their jobs are and influence management decisions to save costs. I understand why companies do it, but I cannot imagine how much money is lost. A better idea would be to talk to the employees and supervisors and hear what they suggest. That way, the changes come from the people who will be implementing them.

Chapter 23

Process Improvements

I was recently involved with one of these programs; honestly, it was the longest six months of the three years at the bank. Each day was harder than the next. I don't think it was actually the program but the people who delivered it.

The company the bank purchased the program from recruited employees to be the teachers and deliver a product that would help save the bank money. One of the methods was a daily graph that displayed smiley faces representing how we felt today. Really? So each day I had to ask my staff to rate their feelings. I understand the importance of engaging staff and getting everyone to work together, but this was belittling to anyone.

Over the course of the program, we had to participate in exercises that would teach us better management skills. After the meetings, we had to "clap out" to signify an end to the meeting. Not my style at all.

I had a hard time digesting this new reality, but in the back of my mind, I knew it would not last. So after the expense of ordering supplies and countless whiteboards the size of a runway, the dollar signs would keep me up at night. Actually, one of those expensive boards still sits in a box; it was never opened.

So after many rallies to keep the program running and lots of applause to signal an end to meetings, this team has gone away, and we no longer practice the techniques we anxiously worked through over six months. Those boards have become coat hangers, and the endless supplies are sitting in cabinets.

Some of these programs may work in businesses they are designed for, but not all areas benefit. I don't know how you would decide what works, but an open mind by all parties is key to any program's success.

Most of these programs have an impact on your team too. Some, of course, will accept change and adapt, but others will challenge you. You may face a challenge from the more senior members of the team. They know their job and completely understand what needs done to improve the quality and process. It's that generation who have a difficult time accepting that a millennial with no experience and a master's in business is going to come into the bank and change the world.

The key is to open up the lines of communication and talk through any proposed changes, whether your team implements the change or presenting the change. Everyone has to have an open ear and accept criticism. It was harder for me because I tend to defend my honor, so to speak. I had made so many positive changes that I could accept those from people who don't know my business.

I got through it, and in some ways, things went back to business as normal. Did I learn anything from the experience? Of course I did: the Becker way.

CHAPTER 24

Planning for the Future

I try to think of retirement and plan for that day. I'm not looking forward to it right now but know it is in my future. I like to work and like what I do. So many friends and previous coworkers have made the plunge into retirement. I applaud them all and will be excited to do so one day. In the back of my mind, I struggle with it because I cannot grasp where the time has gone. I remember my parents planning their retirement and live through the reality that they never got to enjoy it. They could have done so much more.

When I think about the future, I look forward to the second half of my life. At fifty-four, I say it's only beginning. These are the best years, and my goals are set much higher. I want to be a direct report of our CEO; I want to be recognized by my peers in the organization. This is the time to have your reputation proceed you.

I have laid the groundwork and continue to gain accolades for the work I have done with my department. It is hard work, but playing the game is key. There are many people within my world I have so much respect for; I want to shadow them so I can gain their knowledge.

Over the last couple years, I have worked closely with a woman who manages the department I interact with most of all. I immediately felt a connection and respected her position. I used to hear that she wanted to take over the world. Funny part was, I did too. So we get along just fine.

We worked hard to bring our teams together and make a seamless transition as both team become transparent. In the end, our efforts are all about the customer.

So when she retires in a couple years, I want to become the gatekeeper and manage where she left off. So thinking about who will retire within your network is essential, especially if you have goals set for yourself. Go after it.

I learned if you don't toot your own horn, no one will do it for you. You cannot sit back and let things come to you; people need to know who you are and the reputation you bring to the table.

Some goals we set for ourselves are reachable; others may take time. It's okay to set goals that are not reasonable. Sure, we may want to be part of the royal family, but it won't happen. Think about realistic goals and set long- and short-term expectations. If you work hard, they will come; it take patience.

As I prepare for the day I retire, I know it will involve being a snowbird. Kyle and I will make our goal enjoying the seasons from multiple locations.

For my staff, I would encourage them to think big and begin to have those conversations around what they want to do after they have worked hard for so many years. We live in a different world; few millennials will have a pension to support them. They are become extinct, just like a rotary dial telephone.

If only someone could write all this down so there were procedures for us to follow. We need life lesson books or Procedure 1.1 Version 5. Maybe that would be too easy.

CHAPTER 25

Document, Document, Document

Written procedures are something we do every day. When you buy a new watch, most likely there are procedures on how to work it. That new piece of furniture from IKEA requires procedures to tell us how we put it together. Even in our homes: You may follow a recipe to bake the upside-down cake that Grandma made every Sunday. Our cars tell us how we should drive and alert us when we don't put our seatbelts on.

The same holds true in our jobs and how we manage our team. Each step of what we do has to be documented and updated as new systems and processes are implemented. Just like the cake recipe, our procedures need to be written so someone can pick them up and follow along. The end result is we either burn the cake or we don't attach a correct document, and then an audit reveals we failed somewhere.

At home, our auditors are family and friends. You know if an ingredient is wrong and the taste is off, we will hear about it. Or a good friend may just go along with it so your feelings are not hurt.

Auditors don't have that level of compassion because their job is to look out for the business. If we do something wrong, our business will be impacted. More importantly, it could have an impact on our clients.

It is always difficult to make sure every i is dotted and every t is crossed. But if you have your team read each step carefully and follow along, then you will be able to identify a gap.

In some ways, our lives are similar to a procedure. Early on, the purpose of the procedure is outlined by our parents, and they sure do make us aware of potential impacts if we go down a different path. Procedures can be altered at any time, especially when events dictate other steps to take.

During our Baptism (Sit, Stand, and Kneel), procedures are vocalized as our sponsors and parents are reminded of their roles in our lives. Throughout our Catholic upbringing, each sacrament comes with similar roles and responsibilities. Every religion has a similar approach, if you really think about it.

We live our lives according procedures, and each step we take controls the next. Our failures require a rewrite of the processes we learned early on.

Over the years, I have learned that not every process or control needs a documented procedure. Certainly ones that could impact our business do, but common sense in our jobs may not need to be documented. For example, answer the phone, say thank you, or wish someone a good morning. Those things should come naturally and never require a rewrite, although as we progress with technology, some of these simple tasks are going away. Maybe we should have a document we sign to make certain these menial tasks do not go unnoticed.

CHAPTER 26

Celebration

Going to events and celebrating the accomplishments of others is rewarding. Of course, we are honored to be invited and congratulate someone getting an award. Sitting back and observing is enlightening.

It's always enjoyable to join in recognizing a young person who has worked hard and exceeded the goal set by their organization. Everyone should embrace an opportunity to be among so many young professionals who are the up-and-coming leaders. It is our duty as mature professionals to show the younger generation our appreciation. You never know who is sitting in the room; it could be the person who replaces us in our jobs. It could be the next mayor of our city.

That is what I do when going to events: I imagine who is in the room with me. You know there are people who have done more for our communities but sit silently as others accept the accolades. Some people don't need to be in the spotlight; however, others thrive on it. There is no right or wrong because it depends on your personality.

I think there is a rush to one's ego when you are standing on a stage hearing your name being shouted and the roaring applause fills the room. For that one moment, you truly are a celebrity.

In those special moments, we take our bows and celebrate our success.

We should celebrate life each day. It's one more day we had to make a difference, one day we made someone feel good, and one day we said, "I love you," to that special someone.

Our lives are precious and fragile. Over the years, people tell stories about losing someone who meant the world to them and how guilty they felt for not spending more time with them. How much time is enough time? No one could ever set a limit or come up with a magic number.

It's amazing how fast our days go by; at least for me, it feels as though I just finished the previous day and the new one is starting, although some days, you wish it would go a bit faster. I don't want to wish time away; you should never regret when the day seems to go longer than expected. Because the reality is, we never get them back. Sometimes, I wish we could hit a Rewind button and start over; I could use a Pause button too. As much as I try to plan my day with meetings and conference calls, I leave some time for me. Lately, I block an hour for my lunch and thirty minutes at the end of my day to answer those emails you save to the end (remember the sundown rule?).

One thing that always gets me is people who schedule meetings during lunch. It's not set in stone, but common courtesy would be nice. We should all try to have consideration for our coworkers and peers. Let's face it: During the day, we need some downtime to regroup and set the direction for our teams.

Our daily lives are no different. Sure, I love having plans on the weekend and hanging out with friends, but it's nice to leave one day free. If I chose to do nothing on that day, it's okay. So that is my own point about not allowing our busy lives to take control. That is what causes us to have regrets when time flies by.

Sometimes, when an event is a year away, we first take the approach of having plenty of time; we sit back and don't worry. The planning seems to consume our time, and soon that event is a month away.

I cannot figure out why that happens, and I try to think about each of those months and wonder what kept me so busy. Then I realize why so many people struggle with depression or the sense of losing control.

Those are the people we need to reach out and support, include in our plans, and make sure their alone time is filled with happiness. Of course, not everyone would be receptive, and we certainly cannot force anyone into a situation that would make them uncomfortable.

In these situations, I think about many elderly couples who sit by the phone each day, waiting to receive a phone call from a family member. I could not imagine the pain of feeling so sad. These people who shared so many stories with countless family members are now silent. Families change and grow, and some move away, but we should never forget.

The same holds true for people who travel in their career. Truly, it is a lonely life, sleeping in a hotel night after night and living out of a suitcase that has been packed and repacked multiple times. The worst is eating alone in a restaurant filled with couples sitting next to each other, laughing and talking about their days. The only connection you have is a phone call home to hear what's going on in your absence.

I do like travelling and was on the road for many years. Some good and some bad, but mostly, it left an empty feeling in me.

Maybe that is why today, I enjoy being at home so much. Sure, going out is fun, but at some point, I am ready to go home again. I usually get criticized for leaving events early, but honestly, after a few hours, I need to go home. I make an appearance, which is important. My security blanket is our home. We worked so hard to make it a home. Some people have a house, and some have a home, and there is a big difference.

Home Sweet Home

O ur home is a place to take off your shoes, put your feet up, and relax. We don't care if you take a nap in the recliner, either. To us, that says you are comfortable. Any home should be filled with pictures of family and friends and those special knick-knacks that someone brought you from a vacation or gave you for Christmas. Every home has a story and should come alive with the owners who have dedicated their time to make it perfect.

Some houses sit empty, with a cold feeling that leaves you wondering when the final touches will be added. It's a place to visit but not necessarily welcoming you to put your feet up. In most houses, your time visiting is limited by the hours the host invited you. You never see an invitation with "7:00 p.m. until?"

The home would welcome you in and expect you stay until the lights are turned off or grab a pillow and spend the night.

Every structure has a story to tell. Within those walls were celebrations, times of sorrow, and many conversations about life. Tears were shed, and times of silence left the structure to talk in your absence. Sounds of floors creaking and the mechanics of the house keeping you warm and safe all tell a story. The people before you sat in the same room, talking about similar sounds. Some may have felt the house was haunted, but many stories were created.

Our home is a safe place, and we spend years making it that way. We do that with so many things in our lives. Our office space becomes a second home, and we fill it with pictures of loved ones and funny sayings that spark a memory of an event or occasion we participated in.

In new environments, work spaces have become smaller and less personal. They seem more like a house than a home. Since we spend so much of our time sitting in a cubicle, it needs to be personalized to some degree. If it makes us feel good, then that should transfer to what we do in our day-to-day jobs.

The next time you walk into a house, take a moment to digest the surroundings and notice how it makes you feel. How does it touch your soul? Do the same walking into a coworker's cubicle that is very sterile. Those scenarios are physically different but should touch you the same emotionally.

The expression of emotions is important and truly defines who we are as individuals. Our emotions tell others we care and are interested in what their story tells. When I look around the office and observe the different workstations, the array of messages is overwhelming. Some employees choose to display family photos or funny sayings taken from a comic strip. Other individuals fill their space with religious sayings and prayer cards. Obviously, those people are spiritual and find strength in knowing they have God looking out for their well-being. Or they pray for me; I could use some extra Hail Mary's (Sit, Stand, and Kneel).

I like to see the individual expressions and the variety of stuff employees use to make their cubicle a home. My favorites are the calendars with a countdown to retirement (although for some, that is a long way away). Vacation photos are cool too.

So no matter where you call home, it's important to personalize your space. It welcomes people in and sparks conversations. Somewhere, there is a story being told.

CHAPTER 28

Observations

often sit in traffic and wonder about the person beside me at the red light. I try to imagine what they do for a living or where they are headed. Sometimes, I look over and smile; other times, I give a quick glance just to see their face. I do the same walking through the city and looking into the windows of buildings. Who works there? Does someone actually live in that building? Sometimes, a space that was dark last week is now full of light, and you can see the silhouette of people behind the curtains.

Walking the halls of our building is the same too. On some floors, the conference rooms face the hallway with a glass window, so you can see a meeting in progress. I often wonder what the meeting is about. Everyone looks serious, and the facilitator is standing in front of the room, talking.

Some of the spaces in our building have no windows to the hallway or outside. Does anyone really know who is behind that door and what they do? My space is exactly that. You enter a door from the hallway, and the interior room has no windows to the outside world. I would never know if the sun was shining or the rain was falling; maybe not a bad thing, since I am at work. But a glimpse of sunlight would help.

I used to joke about wanting a window, and finally my staff purchased a stick-on window with a view of a beach (my favorite spot). One of my trips to Florida, I had a picture taken of myself pretending to peek through a window. Now a cut-out of me appears looking into my workspace. I always tell my staff that I keep my eye on them when I am not in the office.

We all need to have a work-life balance and separate ourselves for a bit. This is easier said than done, but it's important to step away and re-energize. In some businesses, it is a requirement to completely log off for one week. I certainly agree but find that hard to do. In that situation, it really takes discipline. I tend to check email when I am out, mainly because I know how many messages I get each day. Most can wait, but there is always that one "ASAP" (a term that is like nails on a chalkboard for me).

Those four simple letters spark fury in me, for some reason. Maybe because most people use those four letters to influence you to work harder or to push their weight around. I usually make the sender understand that you can ASAP me all you want; it won't make it any quicker. People need to use common sense and think about what they are asking for. Sure, some things can be done quickly, but most need assistance from others.

In any event, we do what we can and provide a response that is timely for everyone involved. Step back, consider the source, and move forward with your response. To me, if someone is ASAP-ing you, then at least they could call you on the phone.

But in the end, most of us rush to work on a request, and most times, we get an answer before one was expected. It's in our nature to succeed and keep people happy. It does not hurt to let someone know that those four letters are meaningless to you, but of course, do it professionally. Set the tone for how you want to be treated and what your expectations are for them. They should do the same too. Each of us has the right to be treated fairly and with respect.

Having an open mind helps. We need to hear suggestions from others, because it will help us grow and become stronger people. You cannot shut people out, but some do because they feel it's their way or no way. But that's not true at all. Even in our darkest times, we need others to give us ideas on how to pick us up.

Sometimes, people tend to hold in their emotions until they reach a breaking point. No one ever really knows what other people deal with in their day-to-day lives. Most feel those moments are private and should not be shared. I get that.

One of my employees shares many aspects of her life with me, almost every day. There are times I say nothing and just listen, because I know she needs that. I never share her stories, which builds her confidence in me. Those moments are private, and if I can offer an ear to listen, I will do that.

There are times as manager we are put into this position with our staff.

Our first reaction is to walk away and not spend the time, but we should when the opportunity comes up. Some folks don't have the ability to talk to a family member or an outside party. There are days that the weight of employee heartaches weigh heavy on my shoulders. It's not easy, and those stories stick with you. But you know what? I would not have it any other way.

Friends recently got together for lunch, and we laughed about our lives and how we would change it if we could. We joked about moving into a double-wide together and living happily ever after. My own request is at least a gravel driveway. How simple could we truly make our lives if we had to? Do we really need all the stuff we have? Sure, it's nice but not necessary. That's what's called keeping up with the Joneses.

I look around and wonder what it would be like to have the basics. Could you do it?

CHAPTER 29

What Defines Happiness?

C an we honestly say we have reached true happiness? Some people can
say it, but are they really being honest? When do we reach that level,
do we always want more? I think it is more want than need: all part of
downsizing and taking inventory of where we are in our careers and life.
I know for me I don't need more, but honestly, I want more, especially in
my career until I retire. Personally, I want to achieve more in my personal
life. I want to travel and experience new things, see new cities, and share
memories with my partner. I want to make that a goal in the second half
of my life story, volume 2.

I need to accomplish the goals that I set for myself. So the definitions
vary from person to person. If you think about yourself, I am sure you can
apply the same concept.

As children, we need our parents to teach us. We want to become
adults and have the freedom to live our lives. Eventually we strive for our
independence.

Moving into our new home last year, I remember packing boxes and
looking at each item and questioning, "When is the last time we used
this?" Soon, the toss pile began to grow. I thought about the time when
we purchased the item and realized there was a reason I needed it. Now
that it sat in a drawer for ten years, I now cannot justify why I would want
it anymore.

Those decisions are an impulse and our minds dictate the 'need'. It
happens at work too.

I am always willing to provide the tools that help us do our jobs better, if the cost is justified. If we provide outstanding service to our customers, then the cost was worth the investment. The same holds true when hiring new employees. Sometimes, you have to reach deeper in your pockets to get the best you can get. Everything comes with a price, and we need to be willing to pay for it. At the end of the day, our need is greater.

It's like that first car we ever bought. I remember going with my father to the Buick dealership near our home and looking at used cars. The first one that caught my eye was a blue Chevy Monza hatchback. The interior was black leather (well, probably "pleather," but in my mind, it was leather). It had a blue pinstripe down the side. How cool was that?

After a test-drive, we went into the showroom and talked to the salesman about monthly payments: my first experience with realizing I would have to make payments for four years. I was working and living at home; I knew I could afford it.

The salesman asked me, "How much are you putting down?"

I gave him a blank stare because I had no idea. Before we left to look at cars, my father told me to bring my savings book from my bank. As we sat across the table from the salesman, Dad asked me to pull out the book and see what my finances looked like. After carefully reviewing my numbers, I decided on an amount, and we began the endless paperwork of buying a car.

Of course, this came with responsibilities. I told my father I needed the car for work, and I could drive myself to school too. I wanted the Monza, so now I had to agree to follow the rules set by my parents. Those included helping to run errands, picking up family members, and most important was finishing my education and eventually being independent. Oh wait, I had to pay for insurance too. Was that in the payment coupon book? I must have missed it. But that is what it took, so I agreed.

Every weekend, I would wash my car, clean the inside, and detail every inch of it. I got that from my father. Even today, I love buying cars and taking care of them. Of course, my taste has change and surely my passbook savings account has been closed.

CHAPTER 30

Work Ethic

When did we lose our work ethic? It's sad to visit places and see that the quality of some establishments has truly declined, from the simple fast food restaurants to that favorite clothing store we used to visit.

I recently went to get a salad from a local fast food restaurant and was immediately taken back by the staff waiting on customers. One of the clerks had her back facing the line and proceeded to carry on a conversation with the one young man waiting on customers. In between taking orders, the young man was texting his friends. The line was out the door, and needless to say, people were getting frustrated.

One person (I assumed it was the shift manager) was working hard, filling orders from the drive-through and making sure hot French fries were ready to go. Neither of the two individuals at the register made an attempt to help. Actually, the young man taking orders would turn his back and watch as the shift manager ran from one end to the other.

The restaurant itself was dirty; trash cans were filling over with garbage. I gave my order and stepped aside to wait. After I received my salad, the young man walked away to take a break. The young woman with her back to the line finally had to turn around and take orders, and she seemed put out by doing so.

This is not the only example of this behavior; our society needs to return to the old work ethic. I am sure if one of these individuals were actually in the line waiting, they would certainly complain.

I felt badly for the shift manager, who clearly was working so hard to keep up with orders. At one point, she slipped on the floor and almost fell. The floor behind the counter was filthy.

This is a clear example of employees who have no respect for their supervisor or the establishment they worked for; they were only there to collect a paycheck and do a minimal job.

Respect is something we earn, and if you don't demand it back, then you lose control quickly. This supervisor did not have confidence in herself to lead the shift and direct the workers to where they needed to be. But is that really her fault? No.

The manager of that location should provide sufficient training for the team. If directions are not clear, then that manager is not providing sufficient training. As leaders, we should make sure the individuals representing us can do so alone. It comes back full circle; if they are not doing their job, we did not do ours, either.

Whether you call it goal setting or coaching, the interaction with your team is key. In this situation, the restaurant owner is also at fault. Hiring the right people makes a difference. Some businesses fail because of poor management and the lack of good workers.

It is a shame that the art of good customer service is slipping through our fingertips. In all types of industries, there seems to be a decline.

If you think about it, technology may have a lot to do with it.

Even when you call your credit card company, the endless prompts to speak your response is annoying. I find myself yelling the answers into the phone; I said, "No," and then the recorded message says, "Did you say hello?" For the love of God.

The best part is, no matter how you answered those questions, you repeat them again when a live person comes on the line. Where is the time savings? Most calls are then routed to another country, and the foreign-sounding individual says, "My name is Bob [or Tina]." I don't think so.

CHAPTER 31

Outsourcing Jobs

I understand the need to outsource for some businesses, as there is a benefit and a cost savings. But from a customer service standpoint, I struggle with the practice of doing so. Bob or Tina probably never worked for the establishment they are representing on the phone. In training, I'm sure they were shown pictures of the store's logo and a building in the United States. Maybe someone from the corporate office delivered their new hire training; most likely, that was done via the Internet.

Bob and Tina are given a script to have on hand for various calls they receive. The script outlines scenarios that should help them with customer inquiries. It's certainly not Bob or Tina's fault if they cannot help the customer if the issue at hand is not outlined on their script. Bob and Tina need a job too.

After countless questions and repeating the reason for a call over and over again, the call is then routed back to someone in the country where the business is established. This entire practice is outrageous and serves to influence the consumer to shop elsewhere.

Within our own employers, I am certain we observe behaviors with similar outcomes. Not necessarily the same as Bob and Tina, but partnering internally to help a client sometimes lacks commitment to get to the root cause. We tend to pass things off to other areas, when we either feel the issue is too large to fix or don't have the time to be bothered. Neither is a good excuse.

In any form of customer service, there is an end result that we need to adhere to, and that is making our customers feel respected and provide resolution.

Good customer service means you are attentive, are committed to resolving the problem, and follow up to ensure the customer is satisfied.

We had an issue when moving into our new home. The refrigerator was not working properly, and it was under warranty. After multiple attempts and answering countless phone prompts, a service technician finally came to the house. Long story short: It took three visits until the issue was fixed, but now the fun part begins.

Each technician quoted a different price, and in the end, we paid nearly $500 for a part on a ten-year-old appliance. So after the last bill, we called an 800 number and got Tina. Oh boy.

Poor Tina was out of the country but did her best to understand the problem. She was obviously not familiar with the products or services the retailer provided, and I know she knew nothing about refrigerator repair. It took several calls back until Tina finally understood and escalated the issue to her supervisor.

Over the course of these discussions, we were told someone would call back in twenty-four hours with an update. That never happened. Not just once, but multiple times. This is a perfect example of setting an expectation and not following through. When you promise a customer you will follow up, then you should.

It's difficult to understand how individuals would accept this type of behavior as normal. I know I hold my team to a high standard and expect that if they commit to following up, they do, and within the time they commit to. We really need to take a stronger hold on where we are headed.

CHAPTER 32

Giving Your Best

When is your best not good enough? I remember that phrase and think about it often. We all want to be the best at what we do, either at our jobs or in our personal lives. Is the best enough? I think we get comfortable and accept the standard and sometimes fail to reach our full potential. It's not required to be better, but it's a goal to set for ourselves.

Many people get in a comfort zone and feel that they have gone as far as they can and accept it. Why? Maybe it's the drive to move on or it's a security blanket that we cannot let go of and accept change. Some people don't accept change well and struggle with it. These days, it seems like we have to accept it and move forward. If we don't, then we are left behind and struggle to exist in this new world.

Without change, we would never learn; our lives would become routine. In some ways, that just seems boring to me. Try new things, experiment with ideas, and get a little crazy on occasion. Okay, not too crazy, but do something you've never done before.

I'll be honest: I have my limits, but now, in the second half of my life, it's time. I don't really know what that means, but I do know I look forward to a fresh second start.

I'm not going to jump out of a plane or anything (sorry, Kyle). But I encourage others to do what they've always dreamed of doing. I want to see more of the country we live in, travel to states I have never gone to before, take in nature, and explore.

For so long, I feel I have just settled for normal, the basics, and the same old same old. My favorite commercial is for a casino in Pittsburgh.

A woman driving a limo pulls up in front of the casino and rolls down the window. She then says, "Why settle for the same old same old? Because it's the same, and it's old." I love that saying. It makes so much sense, and it's exactly the reason it's time to make a change.

I would encourage anyone to take the same approach. Don't settle for "It's the way we have done it for years" or "We have not changed the process in years." That's not good enough.

We should always look for new opportunities and expand our minds.

As part of coaching, I encourage my staff to job-shadow other areas so they can gain more experience. It's not that I want anyone to leave me (although they may want to). But it's important to have an open mind to new opportunities. It is a perfect chance to decide where you want to go next; we should all do that if we can.

Anything to make us better.

CHAPTER 33

Saying Sorry

Is "sorry" ever the right word to use? It makes sense in certain situations, but I struggle to use it in some contexts. I find it difficult to use when addressing someone who has recently experienced a death in the family or when a situation arises that we have no control over but we want to offer sympathy that it happened. I don't know what the alternative is, but it's worth stepping back to think about it.

Cards are circulated in the office when a coworker has a death in the family. I read the notes people write and struggle to find the correct expression. Sure, I feel bad that someone has died, but why am I apologizing for their loss by saying I'm sorry? It haunts me to the point I simply just sign my name. The words written in the card are sufficient for me at the moment.

Many of my reps tell clients they are sorry; it comes from drilling into their heads that the customer is always right. I get that the gesture can ease a person's mind or lessen the impact of an issue. In most situations we tend to acknowledge the impact we have made to our clients and sympathize with them because an error has impacted their business.

Go back to the issue with the refrigerator. Tina repeatedly said she was sorry for the poor service we experienced. In that case, yes, she should have been because Tina was the one making commitments that were not followed through. She promised a call back and stated that we would have resolution in a certain period of time. That did not happen.

In relationships, "sorry" does work during certain situations. We have all had arguments with our wife, husband, partner, boyfriend, or girlfriend, and "sorry" was appropriate to acknowledge we acted inappropriately. That simple gesture can mean a lot to someone.

In general, saying "Sorry" to customers can have adverse effect, especially if the situation continues. If a customer is experiencing issues and our only recourse is to keep apologizing, the issue won't be fixed. We are only giving them a string to hold onto until the next mistake. Our reputation is at risk since we never own the problem.

Taking ownership and seeing it completed is what will gain us the most respect. Once there is a resolution, the discussion should not be an apology but a clear conversation of "This is what occurred, I found the problem, and here is how I fixed it." We identify there was a problem and acknowledge a solution. That's what I find useful.

If we know where the issue originated and can pinpoint an individual at fault, then we should have a discussion with that person and perhaps implement disciplinary action. Of course, if we don't know why something broke and cannot identify who's to blame, then we have to correct it immediately and move forward.

Document your successes along the way, and take credit when credit is due. There may be an opportunity to identify a gap that needs fixing, which could benefit multiple areas and help with future problems.

Many customer service centers use a recorded line and announce to callers that their call is recorded for quality control purposes. When issues go in a wrong direction, are those calls ever truly played back? We use the lines to hear how calls were handled, especially if we have an irate customer or just to confirm that we are following our procedures. I encourage my staff to listen too. It's a great coaching opportunity. It helps during performance reviews and validates that we remain professional and cooperate with our customers, both internally and externally.

We are recorded, photographed, and tracked all the time. Our privacy has been limited to the four walls we live in, and even there, some cameras may be watching. Walk up the street and look around you; the number of cameras on top of street lamps, traffic lights, and office buildings is amazing. They are important for security reasons, but if I wanted to scratch my ass on the corner of Fifth Street, I might hold back because I can only imagine who is watching me.

This makes me uncomfortable sometimes. Our cell phones are tracked, and we allow apps to access our locations. Are we looking for trouble? Technology has taken over our private moments, and to my amazement, we allow it.

But there are limits, and if it's our own devices, proceed with caution.

My Fears

I have always had the fear of being alone. My fear is worse when I enter a dark room. Fears come in all forms, and some turn into phobias. Mine is more that I don't like the feeling of being alone in the world, even though I have many who support me.

The fear of the unknown translates into many things we do in our lives: from the first steps we took as a baby to learning to drive a car, or the walk down the aisle at our wedding, and for me that was a fear like no other (at least twenty years ago). Many college students fear they won't find a job; others fear walking into a company for the first time for an interview (not necessarily a phobia, but it could send chills down your spine).

Selling yourself is difficult; keeping the interviewer interested can be a challenge. I remember sitting in interviews and thinking the minutes passing by were hours going slowly. I cannot imagine doing that now. It's a hard sell to be the candidate selected from the hundred who applied for the same job.

I went through that three years ago; when I began the interview process for my current job, the first introduction was easy: a simple meet-and-greet with the hiring manager. I walked down the street to the company's building, only a few blocks from where I was working. It was June and 90 degrees out. I was in a suit, and by the time I walked into the lobby, I was sweating buckets. So I stood at the guard's desk for a bit until the hiring manager came to meet me.

We walked to his cubicle, and I sat while he explained the position and told me about his expectation of the interview process. I knew then it would be more involved than I imagined. After thirty minutes, I was walking back to my building, sweating even more and thinking that was my only chance to make a good first impression.

When I got back to work, I sent him an email, thanking him for his time and expressing interest in the job.

About a week later, I was scheduled for round 2. My only thought was to pray for cooler weather. But the day of my interview, it was 90 and sunny.

This time, my interview was with two people: the hiring manager and another manager who reported to him. I remember thinking, *I got this.* After several questions back and forth, the final question was presented to me:

"What would you do if you were hired for a position and the responsibilities changed after you started the job?"

I remember sitting there and thinking for several moments, which seemed like hours, as both men looked at me closely. I could hear the *Jeopardy!* theme song playing over and over in my head.

My answer came easy, and in so many words, I said I would "adapt." That word was key, and it certainly unlocked the door.

We can never get too comfortable and expect everything to stay the same. If we don't adapt to our surroundings, we will never be granted opportunities that will help us achieve our goals.

I remember leaving that interview and feeling good about the answers I gave. After a couple weeks and two more interviews, the offer came. I adapted well and embraced change. Sure, I barked at a few things, but after digesting them, I made it through.

Adapting to our environment is something we all should do; in some ways, we have no choice: We must adapt, or we will be left behind. Today, we may be leading the charge to implement a new procedure; tomorrow, we may be told that process is no longer necessary. Some things we can fix, and others are out of our control.

Travelling for work or pleasure can always be nerve-racking: delays, bad weather, or just the simple act of making it through security lines. It amazes me; tempers start to flare, and passengers blame gate agents for a flight delay or a weather event that is causing their flight to take off late. Really?

Those types of events, we cannot control, nor can that poor gate agent, who came to work that day expecting it would go smoothly. If they could control the weather, I would start kneeling down in front of them, confessing my sins. Well, okay, maybe not that extreme, but you get my point. You adapt to the current environment and have a Plan B.

Most of those people who become irate want to be in control or feel they have control, but honestly, they don't. When those situations happen and we observe behavior that is completely out of line, it's not a bad thing to thank someone for keeping their cool and remaining professional. I don't know what gives people the right to be so nasty some times. Clearly, something has driven them to be unkind. Regardless, we should stand behind the person who is just doing their job.

CHAPTER 35

Holding Yourself and Others Accountable

Having creditability and being held accountable for your actions is so important. When mistakes are made, it's okay to admit it. Anyone would have more respect for you or your team if you honestly identified an error; the bottom line is, we all make them. No one can ever say they did not. We are human, of course. Early on, we learn to cover up mistakes, but as children, we are trying to avoid being scolded by our parents. So if you spilled milk on the floor, you cleaned it up, or so you thought, but Mom always knew something happened. How did she do that?

The old impulse to push it under the rug seems to apply. As adults, we cannot do that easily, nor should we. We grow up to take responsibility for everything we do, day after day. But in business, we don't always own up. Why?

It could be a simple change in instructions, or you forgot to plan that meeting someone asked you to hold. In some way or another, you find excuses as to why you forgot. But the funny part of that is, you don't usually hear just that: "I forgot." Sure, it is easy to blame the fire drill that happened the day before or the countless emails that you could not climb yourself out of.

Driving toward the root cause can bring to light an audit trail of events that led up to the issue. The best way to dive into something is to start from the beginning. Understand the impact and work your way backwards. In that analysis, you will be able to determine where the ball was dropped.

It may be another person who did not take responsibility for the original issue and passed it to another team. They were not accountable to seeing the issue resolved.

We use logs and data to determine who impacted an issue, which is helpful. It's clear one something is passed from one person to another. The original owners lose credibility when they pass a problem off and say, "It's not my issue," or "My department does not handle that product." The bottom line is, we lose creditability with our internal business partners and clients when things like this happen. People should be held accountable.

The same holds true in other institutions. When you make contact with an individual who is representing a business, they should exemplify that company's values.

Each year, we validate compliance and ethics training, which is important. I don't think people take that seriously enough. Can we have ethics training for everyone? In a way, we retest our ethics every four years when we vote. (Okay, I won't go down that path.)

We almost need refresher courses as adults over a certain age, things we forgot but truly make us better people. It's funny, but in many ways, I think people could benefit from it. Anything to remind us of how our behaviors influence each other and the world we live in.

Everyone is so busy.

The bottom line is, we are not always right and need to listen. Sure, we can express our opinion, but that is exactly what it is: an opinion. Don't judge.

CHAPTER 36

Be Yourself

I recently shared a post that read "I am who I am and your approval is not needed." I loved it. That is what diversity is all about. The bottom line is, we are all people, and everyone is looking for acceptance. Sure, we will have differences of opinion, and you may not get along with your coworker, neighbor, or the clerk at the grocery store. But you will not change that person, so accept it.

Even at work, there are many types of personalities who interact every day. Sometimes, feelings get hurt easily over a simple event or action. At the end of the day, does it really matter? I hear employees say, "I'm going to HR. I don't like the way she spoke to me." In the end, was it so bad? I know there are instances when HR has to step in and defuse a situation, and we can identify when that is needed. I continue to preach about the art of good conversation and encourage everyone to step back, regroup, and simple say, "Can we take this off the floor and talk?"

We all have opinions to express. No one should ever feel that what they suggested is stupid. In every suggestion or opinion, there is something that drove a person to express that thought. It goes back to the root cause. An event or incident caused someone to have the feelings they do. So probe them a bit more and really understand what it is they are suggesting.

In many group conversations, the exercise of writing thoughts on a post-it and sharing them with the team can be productive. It gives everyone a chance to speak out. Businesses typically call it brainstorming. Sometimes, I think my brain has a hurricane every day.

This is another aspect of learning who we are and which road we took to get here.

I remember as a child going to my grandparents' home for Thanksgiving dinner. All my cousins would be there, and we were excited to embrace the holiday season. My grandfather had to build an extension onto the dining room table to fit everyone; it actually extended into the living room. Each end of the table had plenty of side dishes, turkey, and all that goes with it. After our meal, we sat and talked about Christmas.

The cousins were similar in ages but I was the youngest. We would gather upstairs with pen and paper in hand to begin our Christmas lists. Our parents remained in the living room, talking about their secret Santa roles this year.

My grandmother used a shoebox tied with a long string that we could send down to the lower level when our lists were completed. Each aunt and uncle reviewed the list before the final approval was given. So we would hoist the box up and down to do our edits.

None of us judged the other for what we wanted from Santa. We gave each other suggestions too. This was an early introduction to brainstorming.

Once everyone agreed, the cousins would come down from the second floor, and we would proceed to play with the hand-carved games my grandfather made. When that was done, we all bundled up and went for a walk into town. One year, we all squeezed into a phone booth, just to see if we would fit (none of those around anymore).

It was teamwork: working together for a common result. These simple childhood practices regenerated themselves into adulthood. I never really thought about it before, but we have always participated in business practices growing up; we learned them early on and would never know that at our age, we would use a similar method again. It's interesting to me, thinking back.

The same concept holds true with those grade school science fairs. It's like an adult trade show, selling our product to an audience. We write our presentation and practice the delivery and most times use props to illustrate what we are representing. Sure, it's all part of education; our teacher back then delivered a curriculum that prepared us for adulthood.

Reflections

As I have mentioned, I cannot classify myself as a religious person. Sure, I have my beliefs and my spiritual side, but I won't commit to attending an institution that profits from my donations. I get that it's not just the weekly offering but a chance to reflect and pray for others who do have strong beliefs and feel that through prayer, good things happen. I certainly respect that of others.

Each night before I finally close my eyes, I lay in bed and say two words: "Thank you." Those two words mean a lot to me. My hope is they reach everyone who has touched my life. My two words are spoken in silence, but I am certain they reach all who have left this earth. Because each person I speak those words to have influenced me in some way.

I speak those words to simply say I had a good day too. I know it sounds crazy to some, but it is my reflection on how I feel, my religion, a simple act of kindness.

When I look in the mirror every morning, I see the face of a man that others see, although looking from within, it feels as if I am the only one walking this earth among others. I do my hair, brush my teeth, throw in my contacts, and begin a new day.

When I pass someone on the street, I wonder if they notice me. Sometimes, there is an emptiness. Do others I pass feel the same? We all have the need to be wanted and feel special.

If you are in the public eye, maybe you want to be noticed less. I'm not sure how that would feel. Maybe I am looking for a simple thank you, or the person I pass needs that recognition too.

It may sound a bit crazy, but my thoughts and reflections are what I feel and believe.

In some way or another, engaging people will be the deciding factor on how well we progress in society and the world. It's not easy, and if we don't work together, it will never happen. We have become separated by political difference, religious beliefs, and influences in our own communities that continue to drive a barrier between us.

It is hard to manage during times like this, and we struggle to keep an open mind. You cannot express your true beliefs and need to keep your personal opinions silent. It's hard sometimes.

No matter which way we tend to gravitate toward, it's all about respect for others. Our country was built on the foundation that we can have differences.

CHAPTER 38

My Mom

On occasion, my mother would host card parties in our home. Actually, there were two groups of woman who filled twelve chairs in our living room. I can picture the three card tables, with four chairs tucked in neatly. She would have place settings ready, and of course the dining room table was set for the after-game pastries. My sister and I would typically go up to bed early those nights and listen to the conversations from the top of the stairs.

One group were neighbors (and a fill-in if someone was unable to attend).

The other group were long-term friends who enjoyed getting together and catching up on their lives.

I don't think either group really did much card playing. But it was interesting to hear the rumble of conversation throughout the night. My sister and I greeted everyone when they arrived before heading up to our vantage point upstairs. The ladies typically came dressed in the skirts, heels, and matching accessories.

The conversations usually involved lots of laughter, and there was always one voice that could be heard over the others: It was my grandmother, who lived down the street from us and was usually invited to join both groups. She was a remarkable woman with a sense of humor that lit up a room.

In those days, the group was free of judging each other; everyone was accepted, and their opinions did matter. They listened to what others had to say, and if someone disagreed, it was accepted. The conversations about religion were limited to what social events were happening at our local parish or the upcoming holiday choir schedule. They sometimes discussed the previous Sunday's sermon.

Thinking back on those conversations, they never took the tone of judgment or jealousy and never had political undertones. It was good, clean fun and the celebration of friendships.

I actually still have the card tables. The funny thing is, when you flip them over, written in black marker in my mother's handwriting is our childhood address and phone number. It's like Tupperware; once you own it, you never want to lose sight of it.

My mother was building her network and making sure to keep those connections available. She was bringing those people together who she knew would support her throughout her life. The gesture of kindness and dedication can open many doors. It's all in the greeting.

CHAPTER 39

A Simple Gesture

The outward gesture of a handshake or the outward motion of a hug says so much to the person on the receiving end. When my sister and I would greet the card party ladies, we would hug each person as they came into the door. It was a welcome sign. We were glad they came.

Generations before us, deals were closed with a simple handshake. There were no signatures or formal contracts to be written. The touch of a hands sealed the deal.

The art of doing business has changed so much; we are so worried about legal action being taken on anything we do. Paper rules. Read the fine print. Do any of us really read every paper we are presented with when signing for our new car or mortgage? It's overwhelming, and the legal verbiage means nothing at the time. I realize companies have to protect themselves. No one can agree on a handshake anymore.

Have we lost trust in each other, or have businesses become so afraid of legal action that they add words into contracts that technically have no meaning at all? We get emails from time to time, asking us to acknowledge we agree to a change with a simple click. I do it, and I'm sure many others do it too. But what does that gain us?

The business world is difficult enough without all the red tape. But within some obscure language in a contract, there is always a way around it. Are we ever really 100 percent protected?

If we do the right things from the beginning and are ethical with our approach, then legal implications should be limited.

Sure, there will be that one person who feels they were done wrong and start legal action to sue. If you follow the trail, most times, the individuals making those claims were actually in the wrong to begin with. No one wants to admit that, so we defend our actions and settle. Some say it's easier that way.

In some of the worst criminal cases, the perpetrator rarely just admits, "I did it." So we spend countless money on trials, publicity, and news coverage to prove their innocence. In the end, they're found guilty anyway.

Take responsibility for your actions and behavior. Admit you're wrong and make it right. We cannot change how people act, but it goes back to a root cause of their upbringing.

Let's work on us and dig a bit more into the root cause.

CHAPTER 40

Setting the Right Price

I s $1 the right price to let a memory go? We recently helped our elderly neighbors Connie and Jim with their estate sale. We spent the night staging the remaining items they chose not to move with them: boxes of holiday decorations, vases, clothing, and furniture. As we began pricing in preparation for the sale, the couple began to discuss how much they should ask. Of course, we stayed neutral and did not offer an opinion because they were their memories.

After the sale started, many people made offers lower than the asking price, typical for an estate sale. At some point, the couple would need to decide a price that was reasonable. But every item they sold had a story.

In some ways, it was sad to allow their memories to go into hands of someone new. Would the person buying that ornament understand the feeling that went behind the initial purchase? A vase that sold for $5 held countless arrangements of flowers, celebrating anniversaries and birthdays.

I noticed the expression on Jim's face as he watched their items pass to other hands. It was difficult for him to admit it was time to downsize, as their new home didn't have room for all their treasures. But in some ways, it was rewarding to know the memories would live on. Someone would share their memory of purchasing these items, and a new story would begin.

So memories of the past live on, as long as that $1 item is cherished by the new owner. It's hard to let go of our belongings, not knowing if the next person would honor them. Sure, the money is rewarding, and we cannot hang onto to our possessions forever, but letting them go is a gateway to a new start.

After two days of the estate sale, we helped take inventory on what remained. It was mostly mismatched pieces and holiday decorations, which would end up in a consignment shop. Clearly, these items were once replaced by something new and hidden on a shelf, collecting dust.

Taking inventory of what we need versus what we really want is a daunting task. But keep in mind that if we placed that item back on a shelf and never used it again, it was time to let it live in a home that would cherish it forever and begin to tell a story of how they purchased it.

Influences in My Life

So many people have inspired me in my life so far. My parents taught me to be who I am today; my sister Kathleen and her husband Tim have proved to me that family is important and should remain a bond that brings everyone together, in good times and bad. Kyle proved to me that I am a strong individual with a voice that needs to be heard and that love comes in many forms; we should embrace what we believe. Other friends have touched my heart along the way, and they have become close to me throughout the years. Susie will always have a special place in my life, as I seem to connect so well with her; her inspiration has taught me to keep my chin up and follow my dreams. Never give up, and when you are thrown a curve ball, catch it and throw it back. The next hit will be a home run. Her husband Jim has given me the drive to succeed in my career and set the bar high.

One person has been part of my life for seventeen years and has filled a gap that no one can. Being an orphan has been easier knowing Barb is looking over my shoulders. Her gentle voice, the wisdom she shares, and that gently touch on my shoulder reminds me of my own mother. She has guided me through good and bad times but never judged me for mistakes I made along the way. I am fortunate to have Barb looking out for me forever. Lum too.

No matter where we go with our lives and the struggles we run into, the people who mean the most will always show support for us. These individuals are part of your inner network, and keeping them close is important. Sure, we have seen friends come and go, but the ones who have remained true are special.

In a dark time during my career, I met someone who saw potential in me. Susan gave me a chance and helped me prove that I was going to succeed. For a couple years, I worked for Susan, and we soon became close friends. We shared dreams and looked to each other for support, and that will never change.

From the beginning, we are programmed with our lesson plans of life. Some lessons are easily taught, and others come to us throughout our years of life. We can never be totally prepared for what comes our way, and certainly no one can predict our futures. However, the path we chose can lead us to our ultimate goals, if we work hard and remain focused.

Think about those pot holes along the way. We temporarily take a detour or repair our egos, but eventually, we get back on track.

My concerns for the future come from our current environment. It's important to get involved, and if you are able, help mold the individuals who will replace us some day. Our parents did that their entire lives. They provided us with a framework and gave us the resources we would need; there was never a training manual to help answer questions. We had to find the answers for ourselves.

Communication is the most important part of anything we do. It comes into play in our personal lives and at work every day. Put the phone down and look at the person next to you on the park bench, or the clerk waiting on you in the store. You never know who that person could be.

Social media plays a huge role today; we cannot escape it. Make the right choices, and proceed cautiously. The world does not need to see what you ate for dinner, nor a photo of you in a hospital room. Remember, besides your friends, others are watching. I vow to change my habits using social media. It's time to take back control.

Family is the most important part of our lives; we should treasure every event and special moment we share. Get back to Sunday dinners and social gatherings. We can learn a lot from those old stories of growing up.

The special people in our hearts will always remain there.

Our jobs are important, and setting expectations for our careers is critical. Take ownership of what you want and work on being the best.

All in all, our lives are so short. If you live to ninety, celebrate the accomplishment and share the path you travelled.

I welcome the opportunities ahead and cannot wait to write about it. The best has yet to come.

CHAPTER 42

End of the Day

After the sale was over and our neighbors went to their new home, the front door was securely locked behind them. The rush of the estate sale was over, and the remaining items remained in the home. Some were on tables, others on the floor; most had their price cut in half in a last effort to make a sale.

We checked on the house for our neighbors; as we opened the garage door, it was clear this once-vibrant home now was just a house. The memories that were shared over the years with family were gone. Even the air had a new smell. It was very strange at first, but I understood.

Someday, this structure would become a home again. New owners will add their sense of color and style to these empty walls. Family dinners will take place, and a Christmas tree will someday stand in the front windows.

Our brains take over, and we imagine people living in this space someday. We imagine dinners and cocktail parties on the deck. It's like our own sense of security and hope for the future.

It's healthy to imagine what will be some day.

When I think of managing staff, I find myself imagining what would be different if I only changed one thing we do today or if I had hired that one person I was not really sure about. So we gather our thoughts and begin to have an intuition of how we want things to be. It does not always work out like we plan, but at least we have practiced it over and over in our minds to accept what did not occur.

Most of us are familiar with a project plan. It is used in all sorts of businesses and in projects we do at home. It's important to identify the projects that are priority and categorize them based on necessity. When you do that, you often find that what you thought is a priority really should be lower on the list. Another approach is identifying necessities and making those your top priority.

For our neighbors, their project plan would have been which items are higher priced compared to those that held less personal value, or which pieces of furniture would make more sense to sell.

Project plans certainly come in demand for projects we do in our jobs, especially if we are implementing a new process. Project plans should also include financial impact.

When we moved into our new home, we created a to-do list and categorized the items by need. It was also fun to put items on a wish list. Those items are fun to have. Not sure the pond I wanted is a necessity or priority; it's certainly a wish list item. It's fun to dream.

As I reflect back to the estate sale and walk through the neighborhood, there is a sense of isolation. Now on either side of us is a house that sits empty. It's an eerie calm.

An occasional light comes on in both houses from a timer that was set by their owners. So for a specific period of time, there is a sign of life. The electric sparks a bulb to welcome anyone who enters in the dark.

Season Comes to an End

I never like to see the summer come to an end. The idea of it being light outside until nine o'clock is refreshing. As we move into autumn, the daylight becomes shorter, and soon the dark of night comes earlier. It's refreshing to know the true meaning and understand why we have seasons. The fact that nature needs to rest and rejuvenate is amazing.

We have now lived in our home for a full season, which is rewarding to me and a huge accomplishment. Moving in last fall was like unwrapping a gift from nature. The leaves covered the ground, and we weren't sure what lived beneath the soil. As winter came upon us, our project plan included many days of painting and looking out into the courtyard, dreaming of what it would become in the spring.

Soon the ground thawed, and eventually, what was hidden began to come up from underneath the mounds of dead leaves and dirt. I remember each day looking out and seeing something new come to life. It was like the house had sat for many years with no one living in it. Now a home, it was time to blossom. The life cycle is truly something to observe up close.

In our families, we see our siblings grow up and become adults with children of their own. I watched my niece and nephew grow up and become adults and begin to build their own lives. Like nature, they took time to rejuvenate and finally blossomed into amazing human beings.

Now I watch as they begin to plan weddings and their futures. So the next generations will begin and keep the family going for many changing seasons.

We try to prepare our children, siblings, and young adults to transition into the next seasons of their lives. Of course, we cannot be there for every leaf that falls or snowflake that melts away. If you compare the seasons to our lives, we follow a similar path.

Some families keep the family name alive for many generations. It's important to them to maintain the family name.

I understand that we want to maintain our family name, but the history has more meaning to me. Those cherished items we have kept from generation to generation hold more value. Of course, we cannot keep everything, but those items that mean the most should remain with us forever.

I have held onto a few items over the years and think about their journey. My father and grandfather collected trains, and I proudly display them in our home today. When I think about when those trains circled around a Christmas tree and the happiness they brought to my family, it brings a smile to my face.

The joy I feel looking at those trains is the same joy my grandfather and father felt when they first connected the transformer and started the locomotive down the track. That is a true memory.

CHAPTER 44

Memories to Last a Lifetime

What type of memories will our young generation share some day? If they don't communicate verbally with each other, will the excitement of a Christmas morning become expressed with a text or selfie? The personal touch of finding the right gift is now a rush to simply get it done.

The only way to know what someone would really treasure is to know them, understand their feelings, and have a sense of what makes them happy. I admit that gift buying has become easy by purchasing a gift card because in some ways I don't know what to buy. Or it's easier to get and allow the receiver to buy what they need.

As a kid, I remember my grandparents giving us each a box filled with underwear, socks, T-shirts, and $20 to buy something extra. Every year, I could count on that box. Although routine in nature, I was excited to open it.

My parents always surprised my sister and me, although we did do our share of peeking in the closet when they were gone. I think Mom finally caught on and wrapped our gifts immediately. We would shake each box and try to imagine what was in it. Usually we would be pretty close, but there was always a surprise that we missed.

Those were exciting times and cherished moments that we looked forward to. As we get older, those traditions become less meaningful. We begin to go through the motions because that is what we are to do. Maybe making new traditions is the rejuvenation that we all need. What was does not always mean it has to be.

Just because a holiday falls on a certain date does not mean we cannot celebrate at another time. It does not mean our gift giving is limited to those specific days. Gifts come in many forms. It's not always about the fancy wrapping paper or the gift bag we spent time picking out.

The most important gift anyone can give is their time.

Our time is valuable to ourselves and others. We value the time we spend together, and of course, most of us value our alone time. But making time is more challenging for some.

I try to give my staff thirty minutes each month to sit and talk. We don't always talk about a work issue, and I generally let them lead that conversation. Honestly, it is their time.

Whether family, friends, neighbors, or employees, spending time to listen and hear them is so important; it's better than any gift card you can purchase. Maybe our holiday gifts should be tickets of time. Give someone a ticket worth thirty minutes, not $30 to the local department store.

We try to schedule time to meet friends for dinner and invite people over for happy hour, and getting everyone to agree on a date and time is difficult. Everyone has commitments, and their families are priority. But flexibility and patience are important.

CHAPTER 45

The Gift of Giving

W hen does gift giving become an expectation? What is the price limit of a gift? I don't think there is any solid answer to those questions, and we have all read about the expectation for different events. Is it required? Do people judge you for not giving the expected amount? You know people do, and by nature we would. It's all about how we are programmed.

The simple gesture to acknowledge you are celebrating someone's success could be expressed in a handwritten note or card. But again, handwritten notes are something of the past.

Another memory of the past: I treasure the handwritten autographs of presidents my grandfather collected. He wrote to each president and asked them to sign a card in a return envelope, and most did. I have those cards saved in a frame, which hangs on our kitchen wall.

I often wonder about what will eventually happen to our current belongings. Who will end up with the trains or the autographed signatures? Maybe they will end up in an estate sale someday. I guess that is up to my niece and nephew. How many times is something passed between generations?

This home contained a trunk full of photographs, film reels, and slides that were left behind. The dusty, rusted trunk was hidden in a closet. These were memories of the previous owner. I have yet to look at them or even attempt to view the slides. Of course, I would never know what the owners look like. In a way, it was sad to hear their children say they didn't want those photos. Didn't they want the memories, or was it painful to think back to those days when their parents recorded the moment?

Taking time to capture a moment holds so much value because that moment will never happen again. Sure, we can try and recreate it, but it will never hold the original emotions that caused someone to snap a photo or make a recording.

We like to fill our home with photos of family and friends. It warms our heart and defines our home.

When we buy artwork to fill the walls, we gravitate toward artists who help express our personalities. We look at the colors which we try to match with our furnishings and make our wall colors pop. But something has drawn us to that picture.

I purchased a picture for our living room as a surprise for Kyle. We had watched a movie about the artist, and I was immediately drawn to the images she created. There were several prints that captured my soul.

The picture I purchased was a young girl holding a baby close to her. The girl has a sad look on her face, but she is concentrating on making sure the baby is taken care of. What drew me in was her eyes. In some ways, this young girl represents me. I tend to care for others and seem to be the one who keeps things calm. I hold close to my true friends and family and defend my values in life.

So the next time you purchase a picture or look to hang one that makes you feel good, take a close look and tell its story.

Did you ever notice the screen savers people use at work? Some are standard images that were installed on the computer. Others are personalized pictures the owner searched for, because they bring them happiness. Some people use scripture sayings or motivational expressions they feet applied to them.

At some point, those images made that person feel good. We cannot influence anyone to change their expressions; we can only support what they choose.

When I attend an art show or festival, I often wonder what made an artist to create a piece of sculpture, painting, or jewelry. What inspired them. Ask them, hear the story, and understand their feelings and desires.

CHAPTER 46

Special Moments

The inspiration to create something can have lasting results on a person. Some have even brought tears to your eyes. Those touching moments can last a lifetime. With each stroke of a paintbrush or the shaping of clay into a vase, there is a thought behind it. So many things we touch every day create a special moment or feeling.

Oftentimes, the feeling of anxiety takes over, especially during tense moments in our jobs or personal situations. We feel the pressure so strongly that our body aches, and we get a feeling of warmth from head to toe. Some of us turn bright red. I know I do.

Those are the demands that are placed on us; most can handle the situation, but other fall. It's difficult to handle, and we turn to those who inspire us for support. Every moment of anxiety seems to last forever, but once we have ourselves under control, we can eventually digest what led us to this point.

The event which led to our anxiety was an overwhelming moment. An artist is met with deadlines to finish a piece for a show. The clerk at the dress shop is inspired to help customers purchase the gown for a wedding. If that dress is returned, the clerk would feel anxious to help that client again. It's a feeling we have when we anticipate an outcome and prepare for the worst. Most times the outcome is not what our minds prepare to face.

Emotions run in all avenues in our daily lives. From the time we open our eyes until we say good night, can you count the emotions you felt every day? It would be completely overwhelming, and there's no way to capture it.

We should be inspired daily to open our eyes and begin a new day.

Our minds hold the canvas to capture every moment and paint a picture that will last a long time. It's unfortunate that as we get older, our captured moments slip away. Our minds fail to remember what happened today. It's like we have reached capacity and cannot take in anything more.

I see this in my aunt at ninety-four years old. She can remember some moments of the past, but if asked what she did today, there is no recollection. At some point, her mind stops remembering the current day. So what inspires her? I often wonder that. Maybe the fact she wants to live as long as she can, but she will never remember what made her smile today. Does she remember the moment someone said, "Hello," today?

I always said I want to live a long time, but after interacting with my aunt and many others similar to her, I would be sad to wake up to only go through the motions of a day without any memory of it.

Our minds hold so much information and make decisions for us every minute of the day. It's our blank canvas.

Did you ever try to shut your mind off? It's not an easy thing to do. Even at rest, we continue to imagine and have thoughts that drive us to succeed.

It's all about what we have set as our path to follow. Our minds remind us of the goals we have set and tell us what we need to do. We even hit Rewind to make sure that our actions and plans of the day were successful. We cannot erase and redo it, but tomorrow's goal can include anything we did not accomplish today.

CHAPTER 47

Having a Bad Day

What is the definition of a bad day? Sure, there are days that don't go as planned or increase our frustration and anxiety. It's a bad day because we did not accomplish what we wanted to. Things happen, and we have to readjust our plans. Sure, unexpected life events can be categorized as a bad day. We never get a chance to relive that day, so maybe it's not so bad after all.

I have several employees who always say they hate one particular day, and that day is Friday. I don't know why issues tend to happen toward the end of the week, but they do. When I think about why the day is so bad, it's because of the pressures put on us to find answers.

Anxiety levels raise, and we tend to overreact until we digest the situation. It's almost like we need to stop, take a breath, and continue on. We need to rejuvenate our day. We should take a rest, step back, and observe and then respond.

Making quick judgments and reacting on emotion is never the best way, and then we could really have a bad day.

Judgment calls work out in some situations, but certainly not all. We tend to go with a gut feeling or emotion and hope that it is the best approach. Sometimes, stepping back to validate our judgment can save a lot of anxiety in the aftermath of a situation.

It is never easy to just walk away from a situation without feeling a sense of defeat. Never do that. Make sure before you turn your back that you have contributed to the situation enough that you feel a sense of accomplishment.

You can never prevent a bad day from happening; everyone has them. Try to turn them around and really look at the situation. Most are bad because we allow it to be that way. In most situations, the problem can be fixed. It may take time and a lot of energy, but finding the right people to help you will bring results.

When issues happen, you have to keep everyone focused on the end result, whether it's a customer, family member, or friend. Again, it may take some time, but hold everyone accountable for their commitments. Set a follow-up time and date. It works.

CHAPTER 48

Time for Silence

When is silence too loud? There are those times that we sit in silence in order to take in the moment or in a disagreement with our spouse, partner, or children. We need that moment to digest the situation and think how we will react. The silence can be deafening.

Before we react and say more to harm the current situation, it's important to gather your thoughts, step away, and rehearse your response. Sometimes, a sharp tongue can make matters worse. Once we understand and listen to our inner voice, then we can position ourselves to react.

In most situation, the lack of good communication is what drove us to the uncomfortable moment of silence. Sure, we may disagree or have opinions on the matter, and certainly our opinions should be heard. Each person needs to listen and agree on an outcome that makes sense for everyone involved. However, it may not be your original thought, but together, you figure out a reasonable variation.

There is more in simple words spoken than trying to interpret words typed in a message. The context can be misperceived, which immediately causes discomfort. Silence is a good thing once in a while. It's not rude or disrespectful, but an unspoken word can have more meaning at the time.

I have sat in meetings when the leader asks for an opinion for their audience. Many times, I sit silently while I listen to others. You may call it being influenced, but I want to hear their interpretation of that question. There are times we react but don't really understand what we are hearing. In most cases, our reactions are sharp. So take a minute, sit back, and listen. It could define the moment.

Body language also plays a key part in these situations. Have you ever observed someone in a meeting who is faced with one person in the room who continually interrupts the conversation? Immediately, the leader tends to defend themselves and looks across the room with obvious frustration. We tend to tense up; our stance becomes more of a defense.

We do that in our personal lives too. In moments of discomfort or heated conversation, our initial reaction typically is to roll our eyes and walk away: human nature at its finest.

So many situations and disagreements could be avoided if we would just listen to one another and not take on a defensive approach. Listen, we are not always right, nor is the other person. But if we cannot hear each other out, what does that truly accomplish?

It is similar when we have to address issues with our staff. Those conversation are not easy, but once we place the facts on the table and review the concerns, it seems to take on a different approach. I always tell my staff to talk it out.

Flexibility is essential, and whether the outcome is ours to own or not, we need to adapt. We don't always win the argument; maybe it's because our facts don't support what we are trying to convey. After listening to one another and laying out a plan that makes sense, we compromise.

There's nothing wrong with that at all.

The bottom line is, we need these types of situations. We cannot always agree with each other, and everyone has a voice. Business would never survive without compromise. The same goes for our personal lives.

My best advice is to keep an open mind, and don't insult each other with the famous eye roll. Sit back and let each other speak their mind in a reasonable tone. In the end, we become better people.

Don't sit in silence for too long because the atmosphere will become uneasy for everyone. You can express your disapproval, but have reasons to support it. If you just reject an idea but have nothing to offer, then it appears you were never interested from the start.

CHAPTER 49

Road Trip

H ave you gone on a road trip recently? As cars pass by, did you ever wonder where those individuals were going or what even brought them to be on the same path? In some of the passing cars, people are laughing or singing along to their favorite song. Some passengers have their shoes off and their feet on the dashboard. Most times, the passengers in the back seat have earbuds in, listening to music or watching a movie. They're probably headed to their favorite vacation spot.

Did you ever notice a single person hauling a trailer behind them with minimal belongings loaded onto it? What happened to bring them to this moment? Those are the people who have a serious look on their face and determination to get home, wherever that may be. They look sad.

I often think how lonely it would be to be a truck driver. That is a lonely life: no one to speak with across the hundreds of miles they travel. The never-ending drive until the next stop.

The conversations in these vehicles vary from basic discussions of what to do on vacation to husbands and wives discussing their family and remembering the last time they traveled this highway. Some remain silent for miles.

The same is true on public transportation. People sit silently, alone, and very few speak. There are quiet conversations in the background as some open up about what they do for a living, usually very generic, as we tend to keep our personal space close. How much is too much information?

I don't think we can ever point to a limit on how much we share with each other; it comes down to what we are comfortable with. If you are willing to share more, then you open yourself to criticism from the other person. We don't want to be judged for mistakes we made or how our lives have turned out. It's all about accountability.

No stranger can ever tell us we made wrong choices. But if someone offers their opinion, we should respect it and listen to what they are saying. Have an open mind. You never know who is sitting next to you.

Start looking around and notice the people who pass by. Think about their journey.

I always struggled with small talk in social gatherings. I find it uncomfortable at times. Maybe it's because I don't know where to begin. In the past, I have tried to look around and pick a topic related to the environment I am in. Maybe it is a simple as "Have you eaten here before?" Or in a private situation, I might start the conversations with, "Tell me about your home." These are simple things, and they seem easy enough, but I find it hard to begin.

Even though I embrace social events, I tend to stand back and take in the atmosphere and observe the people around me. I rarely eat at a restaurant alone or go to a movie alone. That would be so awkward.

I find it much easier to host an event; that way, I feel more in control of my environment.

Taking control of a situation in any situation should be well orchestrated. You need to know the players and have an understanding of their interests. Once you are able to identify with everyone, either on a personal or business level, these situations seem to be less intrusive.

Sometimes in a meeting, a leader can sense their audience does not have total confidence in the content. Identify with those people ahead of time and find a common ground. Call them out, but do your homework. Speak specifically to their job or industry. Having that personal touch can mean a lot, and you will accomplish more.

With social media today, there are many ways to gain knowledge of your audience (but use some judgment).

CHAPTER 50

Inspiration

So many people have inspired me in my life so far. My parents taught me to be who I am today; my sister Kathleen and her husband Tim have proved to me that family is important and should remain a bond that brings everyone together, in good times and bad. Kyle proved to me that I am a strong individual with a voice that needs to be heard and that love comes in many forms; we should embrace what we believe. Other friends have touched my heart along the way, and they have become close to me throughout the years. Susie will always have a special place in my life, as I seem to connect so well with her; her inspiration has taught me to keep my chin up and follow my dreams. Never give up, and when you are thrown a curve ball, catch it and throw it back. The next hit will be a home run. Susie has truly taught me to celebrate life and be thankful for your accomplishments. Her husband Jim has given me the drive to succeed in my career and set the bar high. Don't judge others and be humble.

One person has been part of my life for seventeen years and has filled a gap that no one can. Being an orphan has been easier knowing Barb is looking over my shoulders. Her gentle voice, the wisdom she shares, and that gently touch on my shoulder reminds me of my own mother. Barb has guided me through good and bad times but never judged me for mistakes I made along the way. I am fortunate to have Barb looking out for me forever. Lum too.

No matter where we go with our lives and the struggles we run into, the people who mean the most will always show support for us. These individuals are part of your inner network, and keeping them close is important. Sure, we have seen friends come and go, but the ones who have remained true are special.

In a dark time during my career, I met someone who saw potential in me. Susan gave me a chance and helped me prove that I was going to succeed. For a couple years, I worked for Susan, and we soon became close friends. We shared dreams and looked to each other for support, and that will never change.

From the beginning, we are programmed with our lesson plans of life. Some lessons are easily taught, and others come to us throughout our years of life. We can never be totally prepared for what comes our way, and certainly no one can predict our futures. However, the path we chose can lead us to our ultimate goals, if we work hard and remain focused.

Think about those pot holes along the way. We temporarily take a detour or repair our egos, but eventually, we get back on track.

My concerns for the future come from our current environment. It's important to get involved, and if you are able, help mold the individuals who will replace us some day. Our parents did that their entire lives. They provided us with a framework and gave us the resources we would need; there was never a training manual to help answer questions. We had to find the answers for ourselves.

Communication is the most important part of anything we do. It comes into play in our personal lives and at work every day. Put the phone down and look at the person next to you on the park bench, or the clerk waiting on you in the store. You never know who that person could be.

Social media plays a huge role today; we cannot escape it. Make the right choices, and proceed cautiously. The world does not need to see what you ate for dinner, nor a photo of you in a hospital room. Remember, besides your friends, others are watching. I vow to change my habits using social media. It's time to take back control.

Family is the most important part of our lives; we should treasure every event and special moment we share. Get back to Sunday dinners and social gatherings. We can learn a lot from those old stories of growing up.

The special people in our hearts will always remain there.

Our jobs are important, and setting expectations for our careers is critical. Take ownership of what you want and work on being the best.

All in all, our lives are so short. If you live to ninety, celebrate the accomplishment and share the path you travelled.

I welcome the opportunities ahead and cannot wait to write about it. The best has yet to come.